From
Fiction
to
Film:

Conrad Aiken's
"SILENT SNOW,
SECRET SNOW"

Forthcoming in The Dickenson Literature and Film Series:

From Fiction to Film: Ambrose Bierce's
"An Occurrence at Owl Creek Bridge"

From Fiction to Film: D. H. Lawrence's
"The Rocking-Horse Winner"

The Dickenson Literature and Film Series

From Fiction to Film:

Conrad Aiken's
"SILENT SNOW, SECRET SNOW"

Gerald R. Barrett
University of Delaware

Thomas L. Erskine
Salisbury State College

Dickenson Publishing Company, Inc.
Encino, California
Belmont, California

Library of Congress Catalog Card Number: 77-169710
ISBN 0-8221-0006-1
Printed in the United States of America
10 9 8 7 6 5 4 3 2 1

To the memory of Joseph Conrad and D. W. Griffith.
They wanted us to see.

Contents

Preface

From Fiction to Film is a new approach to the teaching of short stories, films, and the art of adaptation. By concentrating on the problems involved in transforming one medium of art to another, the student, we believe, will learn a great deal about both fiction and film.

The book begins with an introduction that presents the general problem of transforming fiction to film; it then provides the student with an opportunity to put his knowledge to work. A short story is reprinted and followed by relevant critical articles of varying approach and depth, so that the student can read the literary work and consider it from a number of diverse perspectives before he sees the film and reads the critical essays devoted to it. In order to facilitate comparisons between the short story and the film, we have printed a shot analysis of the finished movie. In this way, the student will not have to rely on memory, but can refer to the printed text of the film's dialogue and visuals. Four original critical essays on the film follow the shot analysis. Finally, the book contains suggested topics for themes and term papers. In fact, it may be used as a casebook since it includes the original pagination of the articles and reviews.

We hope that this book will be of value to teachers both of literature and of film and that those students who use it will gain new insights into both art forms as well as develop an appreciation of the creative problems as well as the artistic rewards of adaptations.

Our special thanks for their helpful criticism and thoughtful suggestions go to Professors Herbert Bergman of Michigan State, Hal Marienthal of California State College, Dominguez Hills, Fred Marcus of California State College, Los Angeles, David Hamilton of the University of Michigan, and Frederick Wilbur of the University of Delaware. We also wish to thank Mr. Peter Massardo as well as the Instructional Resources Center of the University of Delaware for technical assistance.

Gerald R. Barrett
Thomas L. Erskine
Newark, Delaware

From
Fiction
to
Film:

Conrad Aiken's
"SILENT SNOW,
SECRET SNOW"

INTRODUCTION

GERALD R. BARRETT

From Fiction
to Film

Most of us, at one time or another, have heard the following comments about a film based on a novel or a short story: "I liked the novel better." "What a lousy film; I'll never read the book." "Boy, did they ruin a fine short story." "This film did the novel justice." Viewers making such statements too often assume that the differences between the art of prose fiction and the art of film are slight, if, indeed, they exist at all.

George Bluestone, whose *Novels into Film* is a basic study of the relationship between fiction and film, suggests that "it is as fruitless to say that film A is better or worse than novel B as it is to pronounce Frank Lloyd Wright's Johnson's Wax Building better or worse than Tchaikowsky's *Swan Lake*."[1] George W. Linden agrees with Bluestone and blames this confusion of two art forms on the average viewer, who sees little difference between a novel and a film: "If he has not read the novel, he will consider himself to have read it after watching the film. If he has previously read the novel, he will either criticize the film for not being faithful to the book or praise it for being a fine rendering of the original."[2] In either case, Linden believes that the viewer's response would be invalid because it is based on an incorrect assumption that novels and films are the same.

Both Bluestone and Linden, among others, believe that a clearer distinction between prose fiction and film would be an important

[1]George Bluestone, *Novels Into Film*, 2nd ed. (Berkeley, Calif.: University of California Press, 1966), pp. 5–6. Excerpts from this book reprinted by permission of The Johns Hopkins Press.

[2]George W. Linden, *Reflections on the Screen* (Belmont, Calif.: Wadsworth Publishing Co., 1970), p. 34. Reprinted by permission of the publisher.

first step toward a deeper understanding of the connections between the art forms. However, two of our great contemporary filmmakers doubt that there are meaningful connections. Jean-Luc Godard (*Breathless*, 1959) expressed in an amazing fashion his concern over the difficulty of adapting a novel to the screen when an interviewer questioned him on the subject; Godard responded with a plan to visually reproduce the physical book on the screen, page by page.[3] Ingmar Bergman (*The Seventh Seal*, 1956) reacted in an even more outspoken fashion:

> Film has nothing to do with literature; the character and substance of the two art forms are usually in conflict. . . .
>
> We should avoid making films out of books. The irrational dimension of a literary work, the germ of its existence, is often untranslatable into visual terms— and it, in turn, destroys the special, irrational dimensions of the film. If, despite this, we wish to translate something literary into film terms, we must make an infinite number of complicated adjustments which often bear little or no fruit in proportion to the effort expended.[4]

Godard and Bergman, realizing the pitfalls of attempting film adaptations of works of literature, believe that it is better not to try than to botch things. We shall see that there is some truth in what they say, but both directors *have* made films based on literary sources. The plot of Bergman's *The Virgin Spring* (1959) was taken from "The Daughter of Tore in Vange," a thirteenth-century ballad read by the director as a university student.[5] Godard's *Masculin-Feminin* (1966) was based on two Maupassant stories, "The Signal" and "Paul's Mistress," and *Pierrot Le Fou* (1965)

[3]Walter S. Ross, "Splicing Together Jean-Luc Godard," *Esquire* (July 1969): 42.

[4]Ingmar Bergman, "Introduction," *Four Screenplays of Ingmar Bergman*, trans. Lars Malmstrom and David Kushner (New York: Simon and Schuster, 1960), pp. 17–18. © 1960 by Ingmar Bergman, reprinted by permission of Simon & Schuster.

[5]Brigitta Steene, *Ingmar Bergman* (New York: Twayne Publishers, Inc., 1968), p. 89.

made use of *Obsession,* a pulp detective novel by Lionel White.[6] In fact, it is hard to find a major living director who has not made at least one film from a literary work. Here are several examples that come to mind: Antonioni (*Blow-Up,* 1966), Bunuel (*Belle De Jour,* 1967), Fellini (*Satyricon,* 1969), Kurosawa (*The Throne of Blood* [*Macbeth*], 1957), Ray (*Pather Panchali,* 1955), Truffaut (*Jules and Jim,* 1961), Welles (*The Magnificent Ambersons,* 1942). While many films by our modern directors are based on original scripts, often written by themselves, it seems clear that a consideration of the relationship between the literary work and the film adaptation is still very relevant because of the number of films derived from literary works that are produced each year.

Estimating the percentage of total film production based on literary works has proven to be a popular and harmless game played by film historians. General estimates have been from 17 to nearly 50 percent.[7] Lester Asheim found that between 1935 and 1945, the major studios derived 17.2 percent of their films from novels alone.[8] Of the 305 films reviewed by the Production Code Office in 1955, 51.8 percent were derived from original source material.[9] In 1967 Harry M. Geduld estimated that around 40 percent of the Hollywood product has been based on literary works.[10]

When one considers the various reasons that directors and producers have for making film adaptations, it is fair to say that there will always be a significant portion of films based on literature, say at least 35 percent. The following review of Hollywood's use of literary adaptations will present these reasons in an historical context.

[6]Ian Cameron, ed., *The Films of Jean-Luc Godard* (New York: Frederick A. Praeger, Inc., Publishers, 1970), p. 187.

[7]Bluestone, p. 3.

[8]*"From Book to Film,"* Diss. University of Chicago 1949. Quoted in Bluestone, p. 3.

[9]Bluestone, p. 3.

[10]Harry M. Geduld, ed., *Film Makers on Film Making* (Bloomington, Ind.: Indiana University Press, 1969), p. 12.

I

Historians have been hesitant to be very specific about the earliest period of the theatrical film, due to the often contradictory facts that have been offered, but most agree that between 1895 and 1905 filmmaking evolved from very short plotless films to crude story productions. The earliest moviegoers were content to see simple static shots of moving objects. When Thomas Edison's Vitascope show opened at Koster and Bial's Music Hall in New York on April 23, 1896, viewers were treated to fifty-second films of sea waves, boxers, and scenes of Venice. Films such as these have their obvious limitations. By the turn of the century, the audience for a film of sea waves and the like had understandably diminished and producers turned to news events, travelogues, and variety acts in an attempt to pep up their presentations. During this period film length changed as well, from fifty-second "shorts" to full reels. (A reel runs about fourteen minutes.) Some have even suggested that several films may have run over an hour.[11] Few films, however, were longer than one reel in length.

There are two technical reasons that account for the limited use of literary sources in films around the turn of the century: first, most films were static camera, single-shot presentations; secondly, individual film length severely limited the literary works that could be adequately presented. Films based on literature were predominantly static documents of scenes from drama. As examples, Joseph Jefferson, the great American comic, played a few scenes from his stage hit "Rip Van Winkle" (1896), and the famous May Irwin–John C. Rice "Kiss" (1896) was actually a short excerpt from a popular play of the time, *The Widow Jones*.[12]

In the early 1900s Georges Méliès and Edwin S. Porter created new techniques that eventually brought part of the lost audience back into the theaters. While Méliès, a Frenchman, worked with a static camera, his films were usually narrative plots that told a

[11]Kenneth Macgowan, *Behind the Screen* (New York: Dell Publishing Co., 1967), pp. 84–89.

[12]Arthur Knight, *The Liveliest Art* (New York: The Macmillan Co., 1957), p. 14.

story: pantomimed tales such as "Cinderella" (1900) and "Red Riding Hood" (1901) gave impetus to the idea of story films. In this country, Porter's "Uncle Tom's Cabin" (1903) followed the directions and techniques exemplified by Méliès. Porter, however, is best known for his early experiments with editing techniques. While the shots were almost always static, Porter was able to cut from scene to scene, showing the development of actions happening parallel in time. The use of this editing technique is of prime importance to the history of cinema to this day and is of major importance with respect to the use of film adaptations of literature. Porter, however, saw little reason to use literary sources for his plots, since copyright laws for films did not exist and filmmakers freely plagiarized from one another.[13]

Still, the middle class in general and the more intelligent viewers in particular were in no great rush to flock back to the theaters to view rather simple narrative films. In 1907, a French company called Film d'Art attempted to draw this group into the general film audience by presenting films of staged plays. This venture was such a success that the company soon found itself turning to novels for source material. Most historians believe that this first extensive use of literary material can be attributed, in some degree, to snob appeal. Arthur Knight explains:

> People who would never have dreamed of going to the nickelodeons to see a cowboy picture, a tear-stained melodrama or a slapstick comedy, somehow felt that movies must be all right if they showed you the classics. For the first time the "right people" began to venture gingerly into the dark, grubby little theaters to see these new "artistic" films.[14]

At around this time, some American producers began to make films of the literary classics, partly due to the lead of the Film d'Art, partly as a response to the growing feeling that many films should be censored.[15] Thus, the filming of a literary classic was thought to

[13]Knight, pp. 15–18.

[14]Knight, p. 21.

[15]Lewis Jacobs, *The Rise of the American Film*, 2nd ed. (New York: Teachers College Press, Columbia University, 1968), p. 76. Excerpts from this book reprinted by permission of the author.

be both marketable and "respectable." However, the credit for presenting an American series of films based on the pattern of Film d'Art should go to Adolph Zukor and his Famous Players Company. In 1912 Zukor purchased the Film d'Art version of *Queen Elizabeth* starring Sarah Bernhardt, one of the leading actresses of the time. This four-reel film was first presented in July of that year in New York City and audiences paid an unheard of sum—$1.00—to see their first feature film.[16] The experiment was such a success that Zukor started the Famous Players Company with E. S. Porter as director. Other feature-length film organizations were quickly started on the same premise; in 1913 audiences were very receptive to the many filmed plays screened throughout the nation.[17]

While 1906–16 is thought of as the period in which the story film gained the ascendance enjoyed today, the production of story films longer than one reel was severely restricted because of a film trust composed of the major producers and distributors known as the Motion Picture Patents Company. This film trust attempted to control the industry from the making of a film to its projection in the theater and had decided that audiences would not sit through a film of more than one reel in duration. Because of the restrictions of the film trust, there were relatively few attempts to make films based on full-length literary works. However, by 1912 the country began to consider the problems of trusts and in 1913 the Patents Company was brought into court as an alleged violator of the Sherman anti-trust law.[18] Thus, from 1912 on, independent filmmakers outside of the control of Patents Company began to make longer films with the knowledge that the distributors of their films would not be harrassed by Patents Company "goon squads," a fact of life prior to that time. This opened the door to film adaptations of a more appropriate length; films could be made of complete novels, plays, and narrative poems rather than scenes from them. Such earlier absurdities as *Hamlet* in ten minutes were seldom repeated.[19]

[16]Knight, pp. 22–23. Also, see Macgowan, pp. 157–58.
[17]Jacobs, p. 91.
[18]Jacobs, p. 84.
[19]Knight, p. 22.

D. W. Griffith's version of Tennyson's "Enoch Arden" (1911) is considered to be the first two-reel American film to be screened at a single showing, but the early emphasis on feature productions came from abroad, where film trusts had never dictated film length, and these films were often adaptations of novels. The eight-reel Italian *The Last Days of Pompeii* (1911) and two 1913 French features, *Germinal* (eight reels), and *Les Miserables* (twelve reels), were early indications of the trend.[20] These continental novel-films were very popular in America, and American filmmakers went on to spend large sums for various novel rights. Griffith's *The Birth of a Nation* (1915), taken from Thomas Dixon's *The Clansman*, garnered the highest royalty of that era. Dixon was paid $260,000 plus 25 percent interest in the film's returns.[21]

D. W. Griffith's place in the history of the film is assured, and one of his many contributions to the medium is the example he set for future filmmakers who wished to adapt a work of literature to film. Griffith became a filmmaker after a financially unsuccessful attempt at writing and acting. At seventeen he was a reporter for the Louisville *Courier*, and he soon took to the road as a traveling actor. He wrote plays, short stories, and poems; his poems and stories were published in such magazines as *Colliers*, *Good House-keeping*, and *Cosmopolitan* and one play, *A Fool and a Girl*, was presented in Washington and Baltimore for a two-week period during 1907 but gained a cool reception.[22] As for his reading, he was particularly interested in the Victorians; Tennyson, Browning, and Dickens were favorites. Griffith began directing films in 1908. Obviously, his literary interests and abilities were richly rewarded in a medium just learning to use the art of narrative. Lewis Jacobs theorizes that Griffith made great use of literary works not for their snob appeal nor for their obvious attraction as "pre-sold" vehicles, but for reasons that suggest the man's faith in the artistic possibilities of the then-infant medium:

> Griffith realized that pictures could become significant only if their content was significant. He therefore led a raid on the classics for his material. Before his first year

20Macgowan, pp. 156–57.
21Jacobs, p. 218.
22Jacobs, p. 97.

as a movie director was ended, he had not only adapted works by Jack London and Tennyson but had boldly brought to the screen Shakespeare, Hood, Tolstoy, Poe, O. Henry, Reade, Maupassant, Stevenson, Browning. Among the hundred or so pictures of this first year were "The Taming of the Shrew," "The Song of the Shirt," "Resurrection," "Edgar Allan Poe," "The Cricket on the Hearth," "The Necklace," "Suicide Club," and "The Lover's Tale."[23]

Griffith continued to "raid" literary sources throughout his career. Since he was considered the master director of his time, one can easily understand why the vast majority of filmgoers thought that the relationship between literature and film was quite close.

By the end of World War I, film had become *the* mass public entertainment. So many films were being turned out to meet the demand that literary sources were ransacked rather than raided, as producers attempted to feed the hungry maw of an industry in search of a plot. Other than in comedy, gone were the days of plotting when someone on the studio lot could suggest a premise and have a group of actors improvise upon the idea in front of a camera (although there are indications that such techniques are presently being resurrected, sometimes advantageously). Writing for the screen was a serious, well-paying profession, and articles on the art of writing for film were written for such magazines as *Photoplay* and *Motion Picture Classic*.[24]

As filmmaking geared itself for industrial output, film adaptations of literary works suffered in new ways. Kevin Brownlow has described the custom in *The Parade's Gone By....* When the work was purchased, it immediately became a property. The property was then compressed into a brief synopsis for a reading by the producer who, more often than not, had never read the work. If the producer liked the synopsis, the property was given to a writer who worked it into a scenario. The emphasis in the scenario was on the visual elements of the work. The property then went through the hands of various supervisors, directors, actors, heads, agents, rewrite men, and the like until a finished product was

[23]Jacobs, p. 104.
[24]Jacobs, p. 219.

readied for shooting. There were "many versions, many conceptions—all of them a compromise between literary convention and cinematic compression, all of them involving further creative blood-lettings."[25] On occasion, even the author of the literary work gave his assistance to the project.[26]

In 1921, Paramount devised a method that, in a sense, attempted to eliminate the middleman, the professional screen writer. The plan was summed up in the following advertisement:

> The greatest living authors are now working with Paramount. Sir James Barrie you know; and Joseph Conrad, Arnold Bennett, Robert Hitchens, E. Phillips Oppenheim, Sir Gilbert Parker, Elinor Glyn, Edward Knoblock, W. Somerset Maugham, Avery Hopwood, Henry Arthur Jones, Cosmo Hamilton, Edward Sheldon, Samuel Merwin, Harry J. O'Higgens—all of these famous authors are actually in the studios writing new plays for Paramount Pictures, advising with directors, using the motion picture camera as they formerly used a pen.[27]

This group was called Eminent Authors Inc. but, as Brownlow explains, "some of the scenarios written by the Eminent Authors have remained in Hollywood legend as Awful Examples."[28] Thus, we can see that filmscripts by committee have severe limitations when it comes to adapting literature for the screen and that there is no guarantee that writers of great literature are able to produce acceptable filmscripts.

With the coming of sound in the late twenties, writing for the screen became even more difficult. In his biography of Irving

---

[25]Kevin Brownlow, *The Parade's Gone By* ... (New York, Ballantine Books, Inc., 1969), p. 311.

[26]Lillian Ross' *Picture* is a fine account of the system and is considered a classic work of cinema reportage. The book deals with *The Red Badge of Courage* as it progressed from a Crane novel to a John Huston film. Many examples of conflicts between writers, producers, and directors are presented. The book is also an interesting example of the factual report as novel, a form that has presently been made famous by Capote's *In Cold Blood* and Mailer's *The Armies of the Night*.

[27]Jacobs, p. 326.

[28]Brownlow, p. 315.

Thalberg, the production manager of MGM until his death in 1936, Bob Thomas discusses the power of the script writer in the early talkies:

> With the coming of sound, Thalberg's relationships with writers intensified. The exigencies of dialogue called for more careful preparation of scripts; no longer could areas of action remain vague, to be interpreted by the director as he saw fit. Now the writer was ascendant, and the position of the director at M-G-M declined.[29]

While dramatic works benefited most from talkies, for obvious reasons, the number of novels made into films did not diminish. The extra dimension of spoken dialogue added to the other novelistic elements capable of being reproduced in the film. The script writer's task as adapter became more difficult and, consequently, he became more important with respect to the value of the finished product. One side effect of this new importance was that the literature from which the films were adapted was treated with a bit more respect, and the films tended to be more successful as adaptations. Naturally, some of this success must be attributed to the inclusion of sound, but the new attitudes about the value of the screenplay could not help but influence attitudes toward the literary work.

The power of the Hollywood studio system increased through the thirties, and, by the forties, the total preëminence of the studio product became a fact of life. The financial strength of the industry, with its increased attendance, enabled such powers as MGM and Paramount to attract many of the literary greats. Fitzgerald, Hemingway, and Faulkner wrote for films at one time or another. With the European disaster of the thirties and forties, writers such as Isherwood, Huxley, and Brecht found themselves in Los Angeles.

In *Hollywood in the Forties*, Charles Higham and Joel Greenberg describe the climate of the time that produced some respectable film adaptations. The studios, feeling financially secure, grew

[29]Bob Thomas, *Thalberg: Life and Legend* (New York: Bantam Books, 1970), p. 165.

more willing to invest money in "prestige" films. The major studios' producers, directors, actors and actresses, set designers, and writers were put to work turning out "serious" films based on literary "classics": "The surprising thing throughout the decade is that the classics should have been exploited with so great a measure of artistic success."[30]

During the thirties and forties, the script writer was often thought of as being more important than the director. Some writers, Preston Sturges (*Sullivan's Travels*, 1942), for example, later became directors on the strength of their script writing. At present, however, we are in the era of the director. Most major directors collaborate with their writers on the scripts; some, particularly the foreign directors, simply write the scripts themselves. Others, to quote the French filmmaker and critic, Alexander Astruc, write with a "*camera-stylo*" (camera-pen):

> This of course implies that the scriptwriter directs his own scripts; or rather, that the scriptwriter ceases to exist, for in this kind of film-making the distinction between author and director loses all meaning. Direction is no longer a means of illustrating or presenting a scene, but a true act of writing. The filmmaker/author writes with his camera as a writer writes with his pen.[31]

This idea partly accounts for the views expressed by Godard and Bergman noted earlier. However, the concept of the *camera-stylo* is an ideal rather than a norm, and it remains to be seen whether literary adaptations, by their very nature, prevent the filmmaker from recognizing his full artistic capabilities in the film medium.

While one might think that such current facts of life as the rise of the international cinema, the young independent filmmakers in America, and the waning of the Hollywood studios would naturally lead to more personal films, that is, more films with original scripts, this is not necessarily the case. What we

[30]Charles Higham and Joel Greenberg, *Hollywood in the Forties* (London: The Tantivy Press, 1968), p. 105.

[31]Alexandre Astruc, "The Birth of a New Avant-Garde: *La Camera-Stylo*," *The New Wave*, ed. Peter Graham (Garden City, N. Y.: Doubleday and Co., Inc., 1968), p. 22. This essay was written for *Ecran Français* and appeared in 1948.

know at this point is that the main reasons for using literature as film sources have been with us since nearly the beginnings of film and will probably continue to be evident in the future. The artistic value and publicized title of the original literary works, particularly novels, are "pre-sold." Also, there are presently a number of examples of a "spinoff" trend, the novel written after the fact of the film; Erich Segal's bestseller, *Love Story* (1970), grew out of his film scenario and its commercial success is in turn helping to sell the film. As Otto Preminger (*Exodus*, 1960) has said with respect to *Love Story*, "There are two advertising media. One is the bestseller. The other is TV."[32] Whether the film is adapted from the novel or, in some cases, the novel is adapted from the scenario of the film, Preminger's point is well taken. According to Joseph Gelmis, some movie companies have helped to make bestsellers out of novels to which they own film rights. Gelmis notes that film company employees were given money to purchase numerous copies of *Love Story*, *Rosemary's Baby*, and *The Godfather* in markets that influence the bestseller lists published by several newspapers.[33]

Aside from the "pre-sold" literary classic and the bestseller as an advertisement for the film, history offers the following explanations for film adaptations of literary works: films based on literature have a certain snob appeal and often are used to bolster the sometimes sagging cultural posture of the industry as a purveyor of art; many who have not read the literary work will want to see the film to catch up culturally; literature offers ready-made plots and themes for producers and directors hard put to come up with an original idea; adaptations offer highly creative challenges to filmmakers willing to take the risk of failure. In most cases, the reasons are undoubtedly a combination of these as well as others of a more idiosyncratic nature.[34]

[32]"Three Gatherings," *The New Yorker* (January 30, 1971): 22.

[33]Joseph Gelmis, "Exhibitionists and the Games They Play," *New York* (August 31, 1970): 58.

[34]A particular piece of literature might be considered a "perfect" vehicle for a particular star (Elizabeth Taylor as Cleopatra). Or, a particular director or producer might have certain literary favorites that he would enjoy turning into films. (Godard has said that he would like to make a film based on a novel by Thomas Hardy. [!])

No matter what reason a filmmaker has for adapting a literary work to the film medium, his decision to do so should lead him to consider the relationship between literature and film. The next section will treat some significant aesthetic theories dealing with this relationship and will outline a theory of adaptation, particularly with respect to prose fiction.

II

Art forms always attract critical minds who enjoy analyzing, commenting upon, and theorizing about the works of the artists. In some cases the artists themselves take on the role of theorists. In literature, John Dryden and T. S. Eliot may serve as examples; in film, Sergei Eisenstein and the New Wave director-critics (Godard, Truffaut, Chabrol) could be seen in the same light. More often than not, major directors, like major writers, do not take on the role of the critic for any extended time; such intellectually stimulating work is usually done by men who consider themselves to be practicing theorists rather than professional filmmakers. However, as in so many cases when it comes to matters of general film theory, one of the first major evaluations concerning the relationship between prose fiction and film was advanced by Eisenstein in an essay written in 1944, "Dickens, Griffith, and the Film Today." This important essay refutes one of three major assumptions concerning the relationship between literature and film.

The film audience has traditionally assumed that drama is closer to the art of film than prose fiction or poetry. Hollywood tended to hold this assumption at least twice during its brief history: many of the earliest story films were excerpts of plays, and with the advent of sound in the late twenties and early thirties, dramatists, stage directors, and stage actors and actresses flooded Hollywood and were given high-paying jobs. As the silent film developed as an art, and as the sound film has similarly evolved, there have been definite moves away from the drama form as a cinema aesthetic. The reasons for this are implicit in Eisenstein's essay, and it is far from coincidental that he finds his proof in the work of D. W. Griffith.

The very heart of the art of the film is its ability to change visual viewpoints of static or moving objects in time and space. This is done through film editing or cutting aided by the moving camera, and Griffith was the first to use all of the basic editing and moving camera techniques with a high degree of artistic control. Eisenstein theorizes that Griffith developed his techniques through his reading of narrative prose, particularly Dickens' novels. The use of close-ups, parallel editing sequences, intercuts, fades, dissolves, camera angles, pans, and tracks can be found in a film such as *Intolerance* (1916), and these techniques are all to be found in novels rather than plays.[35] A. B. Walkley reported the following in the *Times* of London, April 26, 1922:

> He [Griffith] is a pioneer, by his own admission, rather than an inventor. That is to say, he has opened up new paths in Film Land, under the guidance of ideas supplied to him from outside. His best ideas, it appears, have come to him from Dickens, who has always been his favorite author. . . . Dickens inspired Mr. Griffith with an idea, and his employers (mere "business" men) were horrified at it; but, says Mr. Griffith, "I went home, re-read one of Dicken's novels, and came back next day to tell them they could either make use of my idea or dismiss me."[36]

Such an insight into Griffith's use of literary sources accounts for his various literary adaptations as well. While he surely attempted to do justice to the literature, it is clear that particular works were chosen because of the technical problems they presented. For example, Griffith's company, Biograph, was very hesitant in allowing him to make a film based on Browning's poem, "Pippa Passes." The director was most insistent. Given the innovations in lighting that resulted through the aid of his cameraman,

[35]For a description of these techniques, see the introductory material before the shot analysis.

[36]Sergei Eisenstein, "Dickens, Griffith, and the Film Today," *Film Form* (New York: Harcourt, Brace and Co., Inc., 1949), p. 205.

Billy Bitzer, it is easy to understand the attraction of a poem in four parts that would demand lighting for scenes taking place during the morning, at noon, through the evening, and at night.[37] Using literary sources for such experiments, Griffith eventually produced all of the major film techniques. In particular, works of narrative prose fiction helped him to make film a narrative art.

Based on Griffith's experiences with film adaptation of prose, we may conclude the following about film narration. Through editing and the moving camera, a film may jump forward and backward in time, move from one scene to another in space, look at a scene from a distance, shift to a closeup of a particular detail in the scene, and look at it from a number of different angles. Obviously, the drama cannot do all of these things since the viewer is seated at a fixed point in the auditorium and can view the event on the stage from only one angle. Thus, with respect to similar narrative techniques, prose fiction should be easier to adapt to the screen than drama.

The second incorrect assumption held by many moviegoers is that film communicates the same kinds of information as prose fiction and does so in the same way. In *Novels into Film*, George Bluestone addresses himself to this misconception by outlining the different ways fiction and film produce meaning. Bluestone believes that the most obvious difference between film and literature is that film presents a photographic reproduction of physical reality, whereas language alludes to this reality through the use of verbal symbols. Prose fiction is made up of words that are imaginatively perceived by the reader through a thought process, but film demands no cognition since the information is directly perceived.[38] Consider this as an example:

> If I say, "The top spins on the table," my mind assembles first the top, then the spinning, then the table.... But on the screen, I simply perceive a shot of a top spinning on a table....[39]

This difference is most apparent, and quite crucial, when we

[37]Jacobs, pp. 107–108.
[38]Bluestone, pp. 20–24.
[39]Bluestone, p. 59.

consider one of the basic tools of literary communication, the metaphor. Language is highly connotative, while film is not; hence, a literary work that places an emphasis upon metaphor would seem inappropriate as a source of film adaptation. Virginia Woolf has commented upon this:

> Even the simplest image: "my love's like a red, red rose, that's newly sprung in June," presents us with impressions of moisture and warmth and the flow of crimson and the softness of petals inextricably mixed and strung upon the life of a rhythm which is itself the voice of the passion and the hesitation of the love. All this, which is accessible to words alone, the cinema must avoid.[40]

Interestingly, some writers are disturbed about the built-in flux of meaning in language, and have attempted to present the "truth" of reality by eliminating connotation. Given the nature of language, such attempts are doomed to failure, and one suspects that these writers are well aware of this and include such an understanding in their literary strategies. Alain Robbe-Grillet has written works calculated to attack this limitation of language and it is not surprising that his novels have been called "cinematic," that his short story collection is titled *Snapshots*, and that he is presently making feature-length films.

However, most of us would be inclined to think that Virginia Woolf's comment upon film limitation is more telling than Robbe-Grillet's correct assumption about the nature of language. We are willing to live with connotative language because words render a rich imaginative experience. On the other hand, we might wish that the rendering of experience through direct visualizations could be more imaginatively stimulating than it is. This, I suspect, is one of the reasons so many viewers are dissatisfied with films made from great literary works.

This is not to say that filmmakers have not tried to reproduce metaphor in film. Bluestone notes that montage offers the director a unique cinematic tool that can be used for an effect analogous

---

[40]Virginia Woolf, "The Movies and Reality," *New Republic*, 4 (August 4, 1926): 309. Quoted in Bluestone, p. 21.

to the literary metaphor.[41] Through editing, film is able to jump from one action to another and from one object to another, making contrasting comments with somewhat the same effect as figurative language. Still, the effect is analogous but not equal, for words produce richer webs of connotative information than montage images.

Other important distinctions made by Bluestone create this rule: fiction is better able to represent the interior realities of man, while film is more adept at presenting his exterior world. For example:

> The rendition of mental states—memory, dream, imagination—cannot be as adequately represented by film as by language. If the film has difficulty presenting streams of consciousness, it has even more difficulty presenting states of mind precisely by the absence in them of the visible world.[42]

We know of one instance where this view seems contradictory to that rule, the presentation of time. Time cannot literally be seen, but it can be perceived through dislocations of space. Hence, while modern novelists and story writers grow more and more interested in detailing man's interior world, they grow more and more frustrated in their attempts to place man in the flux of time. Here is where film has an edge over prose fiction. Through cinematic editing, double exposure, and the like, we are able to experience past, present, and future simultaneously in space, thus creating the illusion of the time flux. Language, being sequential, is unable to do this.[43]

Given all of the significant differences between novel and film, Bluestone understandably concludes that we have no right to expect the film to be like the novel because "the filmed novel, in spite of certain resemblances, will inevitably become a different artistic entity from the novel on which it is based."[44]

At this point, I should add that this discussion has been proceeding with the understanding that we have been considering the

[41]Bluestone, pp. 24–27.
[42]Bluestone, p. 47.
[43]Bluestone, pp. 48–61.
[44]Bluestone, p. 64.

difficulties inherent in adapting successful literary works of art to film. Many fine films have been based on poor novels: Ford's *The Informer* (1935), Visconti's *Ossessione* (*The Postman Always Rings Twice*, 1942), Nichols' *The Graduate* (1967). No one has ever complained that these films did not do justice to their respective books. In other words, those who invalidly complain that the film was not like the book characteristically feel the necessity to do so when a film has been made from an artfully successful literary product.

This fact of cinematic life leads to our consideration of the third, and last, incorrect assumption about literature and film: great literary works should never be adapted to film because such adaptations are doomed to failure. Obviously, it would be impossible for one person to hold both the second assumption as well as this third. Some err by assuming too many relationships between fiction and film, others, by assuming too few. John Dryden's comments on the art of literary translation found in his "Preface to Ovid's Epistles" (1680) can be used to suggest these positions on translating literature to film. Dryden reduces literary translation to three types:

> First, that of metaphrase, or turning an author word by word and line by line, from one language to another. . . . The second way is that of paraphrase or translation with latitude, where the author is kept in view by the translator, so as never to be lost, but his words are not so strictly followed as his sense, and that too is admitted to be amplified, but not altered. . . . The third way is that of imitation, where the translator . . . assumes the liberty not only to vary from the words and senses, but to forsake them both as he sees occasion; and taking only some general hints from the original, to run division on the groundwork as he pleases.[45]

Dryden dislikes metaphrase, for no language can adequately reproduce another, word for word, and he also dislikes imitation, for this allows the translator to write as a second author, to use the original "as a pattern, and to write, as he supposes that [original]

[45]John Dryden, *Of Dramatic Poesy and Other Critical Essays*, ed. George Watson (London: J. M. Dent and Sons, Ltd., 1962), I, p. 268.

author would have done, had he lived in our age, and in our country."[46] Dryden finds that the paraphrase exists as a sensible middle ground between these two extremes. The translator who paraphrases must be in control of the language of the original work as well as his own native tongue, must find a means of expressing the original as closely as possible without ruining the beauty of his own language, and must take great care that the sense of the original is retained—not part of the sense but all of it.

While we know that film adaptations are not literary translations, let us consider how Dryden's theory may apply to literature and film. Metaphrase is out of the question for the many reasons given by Bluestone; there is simply no way to change words to images as a metaphrase would demand. Imitation is another matter. Many films have been made that could be called imitations. In such films the literary works become "properties," and there is little or no attempt made to render a cinematic equivalent of the original. Such films might use part of the plot, some of the characters, and a theme or two from the original, but there are so many eliminations, changes, and additions that the sense of the original literary work is lost. On occasion, only the title of the original work is retained. Such films may or may not be successful works of cinematic art, but their worth will have nothing to do with their creative adaptation of the literary work. Many film "imitations" exist, and most are failures because the pragmatic reasons for the initial purchase of the "property" often are indicative of the tastes and values that govern the making of the finished film. Naturally, such films make it just that much harder for creative adaptations to be taken seriously.

It follows, then, that the artful film adaptation would be similar to Dryden's idea of a literary paraphrase. Unfortunately this is not quite the case, and it is for this reason that some assume that a valid film adaptation of a literary work is an impossibility. The film adapter could have a control of the art of language and the art of film; but, for reasons previously noted, while he could express some of the language cinematically, he could not express all of it. Further, while he could take great care to communicate

[46]Dryden, p. 270.

a sense of the original, he could not possibly express *all* the sense of the original. It is impossible for a two- or even three-hour film to duplicate a novel taking five to ten hours to read. Erich von Stroheim's *Greed* (1923) is the classic example of the results obtained from meeting this latter problem head-on. *Greed* is an adaptation of Frank Norris' naturalistic novel, *McTeague*. Stroheim attempted to produce a complete film version of the novel as well as some material of his own. The novel is over 300 pages long and the faithful translation produced seven and a half hours of finished edited film. Stroheim's additions brought the finished film up to forty-two reels (ten hours). MGM raged and had the director edit the film down to a more reasonable length for screening. Stroheim reduced the film to five hours; his friend, director Rex Ingram, lopped off an hour of that; and MGM, still not satisfied, gave it to a third party who had few ideas about Norris' novel and fewer about Stroheim's conception of it. The released version was two and one half hours in length.[47] The sixteen-mm rental print runs one hour and fifty-four minutes. It is to Stroheim's eternal credit that the film makes any sense at all! Clearly, the sense of the original has not been totally retained. Hence, even if we were to assume that the experience and ideas in a novel were not ever-lastingly confined by the inextricable web of the language, the conventions of film length are such that paraphrase is impossible.

But what of the short story? (For purposes of this discussion, the novella will be considered as a short novel or a long short story.) Theoretically, the limited material of the short story should enable the director to cover the various senses of a particular story in the length of a feature film. However, this is not the case, for the short story often gains its compression of material partly through a poetic use of language, and, as we know, film is limited in its ability to treat connotative language. Further, while the short story characteristically treats fewer sequences of actions, filmmakers tend to expand plot to the point that the feature film adapted from a short story will contain more original material than adapted material. Thus, the finished film is often "from" or "based on" or

[47]Joel W. Finler, *Stroheim* (Berkeley, Calif.: University of California Press, 1968), pp. 33–34.

"inspired by" the original rather than adapted. Finally, short story–
films of less than feature length run afoul of the very same problems as novel-films.

Thus, using Dryden's description of types of translation, clearly
one cannot translate a work of literature to film. However, those
who assume that the literary work cannot be adapted into a film
assume that the characteristic method of adaptation is translation.
This is not the case. As George Linden suggests, the adaptation is
a *transformation* rather than a translation.[48]

The key to transformation is analogy. Adaptation by analogy,
incidentally, is nothing new, for this is the characteristic way artists
have always adapted a work of art to another medium. Art forms
are unique in the way that they communicate content; indeed,
some hold that the content in one art form is untranslatable to
another because the art form actually shapes the content. However,
as Bela Balazs, the great Hungarian film critic, has pointed out,
adaptations from one art form to another have been made successfully for centuries. The method is the same in all cases, and Balazs
outlines it for film adaptations:

> To accept the thesis that the content or material deter-
> mines the form and with it the art form, and neverthe-
> less to admit the possibility of putting the same material
> into a different form, is thinkable only if the terms are
> used loosely, that is if the terms "content" and "form"
> do not exactly cover what we are accustomed to call
> material, action, plot, story, subject, etc. on the one
> hand and "art form" on the other. There can be no
> doubt that it is possible to take the subject, the story,
> the plot of a novel, turn it into a . . . film and yet pro-
> duce perfect works of art in each case—the form being
> in each case adequate to the content. . . . It is possible
> because, while the subject, or story, of both works is
> identical, their *content* is nevertheless different. It is
> this different *content* that is adequately expressed in
> the changing form resulting from the adaptation.[49]

[48]Linden, p. 35.
[49]Bela Balazs, *Theory of the Film*, trans. Edith Bone (London:
Dennis Dobson, Ltd., 1952), pp. 259–60. Excerpts from this
book reprinted by permission of the publisher.

The successful film adaptation of a novel must walk a thin line between expressing the values of the novel and expressing values that, while artfully done, have nothing to do with the novel. In terms of Dryden's idea of the translation, the film adaptation can be neither a paraphrase nor an imitation, but something in between. The film should not be evaluated on the basis of its faithfulness to all elements of the novel; neither should it be seen as an entity having nothing whatever to do with the original. Through analogy, film can suggest the values of a particular novel; however, because of the many limitations previously mentioned, film cannot do so totally. Hence, it must attempt to capture the spirit of the work. Linden has commented on this point:

> A director can change the plot of a novel, he can elim-inate certain characters and scenes, and he can include scenes not included in the novel without violating it. But he cannot seriously violate the theme of the novel, and the one thing he must be able to translate into his new medium is its tone. . . . Of course, if the director succeeds in his effort, he will have produced not a copy of the novel, but a new object: an art film that aims at close targets in a different way.[50]

Linden suggests that Martin C. Battestin's essay "Osborne's *Tom Jones*: Adapting a Classic" is a fine example of an application of the proper criteria for film adaptation. This essay is well-suited to our purposes, particularly since Battestin is a representative of that profession that too often assumes that film adaptations of literary classics are doomed to failure. He is a professor of English and a Henry Fielding scholar. Further, his credentials are impeccable: he has written a book on Fielding's art and has edited a number of the novels. Too often in the past, such a scholar would be quite hesitant to praise a film version of a work by a writer in his chosen literary field. Naturally, no film would be able to capture the total meaning of the literary work, and scholars have been heard to say ". . . must be turning over in his grave!" or, "If only . . . were alive today to see this!" Thus, the case for the creation of an artful film adaptation through analogy is quite strong when a Fielding scholar

[50]Linden, p. 49.

is able to praise the film version of *Tom Jones* (1963) as "...a splendid illustration of what can be done in the intelligent adaptation of fiction to the screen."[51] Battestin, however, has not closed his eyes to the limitations of the film: he is aware that *Tom Jones* does not reproduce every character and scene to be found in the original; he even concludes that the film hardly captures the moral vision of the novel. However, in Battestin's eyes, the film succeeds in spite of this: "If Osborne [the scriptwriter] and Richardson [the director] missed a major intention behind Fielding's novel, they fully grasped and brilliantly recreated its essential spirit and manner."[52] This cinematic success is achieved through analogy:

> Analogy is the key. To judge whether or not a film is a successful adaptation of a novel is to evaluate the skill of its makers in striking analogous attitudes and in finding analogous rhetorical techniques.[53]

III

Having considered the inherent difficulties of adapting a literary work to film and having constructed a general theory of how such adaptations may be done, one pragmatic question remains: how may one determine the success or failure of a particular film adaptation? First of all, one should have a clear knowledge of what the literary work is doing and how these ends are achieved. In the case of this book, the criticism found immediately after the short story should help to develop an interpretation. Secondly, one should have an equally lucid view of the values of the film and its methods of achievement. Again, in terms of this book, the criticism on the film placed after the shot analysis should be of aid. (Since the shot analysis is an interpretive transcript of the finished film rather than a pre-film shooting script or pre-film scenario, its im-

---

[51]Martin C. Battestin, "Osborne's *Tom Jones*: Adapting a Classic," *Man and the Movies*, ed. W. R. Robinson (Baton Rouge: Louisiana State University Press, 1967), p. 45. Reprinted by permission of the publisher.

[52]Battestin, p. 36.

[53]Battestin, p. 37.

portance will become clear as one works on the relationships between story and film.)

After developing an interpretation of both the story and the film, the next step should be a consideration of the worth of the film as an adaptation. At this point, the basic criterion for adaptation should be kept in mind: a successful adaptation will reproduce as much of the spirit and as many of the themes of the original as possible given the limitations of the film medium. The film may eliminate part of the plot or a number of the characters of the original work; it may even add plot sequences and characters as it sees fit. Such decisions are perfectly acceptable as long as a serious distortion of the original does not result. Finally, one should remember that the successful adaptation gains many of these ends through analogous techniques. While both Linden and Battestin have made this point, it is well to remember that some elements of prose fiction can readily be adapted to film without the need for transformation of the material through analogy. On the other hand, other prose fiction elements cannot be transformed into cinematic devices so readily. To suggest how all of this works, brief comments on the relationship between specific devices found in prose fiction and film will follow. Since several fiction/film devices have already been discussed at some length, some of the comments will be made in the form of summary statements.

PLOT

Since plot in fiction is an artful selection of meaningful representative actions, it is relatively easy to duplicate in a film. Plot usually consists of a beginning, that is, a stasis point, a kind of fixed order; a middle, a conflict of two forces that threaten to break up the ordered norm; and an end, the resolution of this conflict.

Naturally, there are ordinarily many more representative actions in the novel than in the short story. When a film is adapted from a novel, the representative actions must, of necessity, be limited. While the short story usually contains fewer actions, the film adaptation usually is presented in a shorter period of actual screen time, thus creating virtually the same problem as the treatment of plot in the novel; the other alternative would be to have the film expand upon the plot itself. There are very few cases where the film adaptation of a story chooses to present only the actions portrayed in the story in a full-length (ninety-minute) work, most likely because the short story tends toward poetic compression and the film is unable to expand these elements to make up for the limitation of action. Thus, a film adaptation of a literary plot may eliminate some actions and add others, the rule being that the adaptation should be as artfully representative and selective in terms of the raw material of the literary work as that work was representative and selective of the raw materials of reality. Finally, it must be remembered that the basic difference between prose narrative and film narrative is that what the words do in prose the film usually does in images.

CHARACTER

There are two basic characters in film as well as in prose —the protagonist, that person who represents the positive values in the story, and the antagonist, that person in conflict with him. In order for the audience or the reader to identify with the protagonist and feel threatened by the antagonist, the characters must be well-rounded—enough information must be given about them so that they become believable to us. Other flatter characters may surround these two in such a way that a fully realized world is presented. Sometimes such characters are foils, characters who are compared with or contrasted to the protagonist or antagonist in ways that help to define their characters. On other occasions, some of the flatter characters serve to represent particular value systems or cultural points of view that help to make the main conflict understandable. As in our consideration of plot, it is easy to see that the novel can develop a more complex network of various characters than the short story or film. Further, there will also be a tendency toward static characterization in the short story and film for much the same reasons. However, the short story is able to produce rounded, dynamic characterizations through a careful selection of plot incidents and character details as well as through language compression, a tactic that is of limited use to the film-maker. This problem may be partly resolved through analogy:

> The gestures of visual man are not intended to convey concepts which can be expressed in words, but such inner experiences, such nonrational emotions which would still remain unexpressed when everything that can be told has been told.[54]

While the director may be unable to express the wealth of detail needed for a rounded character found in the successful prose narrative, he can make use of the visual dramatization produced by the actors and actresses themselves, something prose fiction cannot do.

Ultimately, whether we are reading about characters or watching them on the screen, their actions and character changes must be plausible (believable), consistent (compatible with their personalities), and motivated (they should act for a valid reason). Too often in the past, film characterizations have not been as strong as those found in prose fiction. This, in part at least, explains the hold the star system has had over films, particularly in this country. Typically, the director is able to use actors and actresses with identifiable screen characters developed over the years. A Bogart, a Brando, a Monroe, or a Loren is able to play a type developed during the course of many films, and the lazy director relies upon typecasting to carry the weight of the characterization. While the star system will always be with us to some extent, the film today is more willing to rely upon the artistry needed to produce a well-rounded character in a particular film. It must be remembered that film is in its infancy relative to the literary arts. In a sense, the history of film in terms of characterization can be seen as similar to early folk literature where types and stock characterizations are to be found in abundance. However, gone are the days of "good guys" and "bad guys" as staples of film characterization. Finally, one other limitation of film characterization should be mentioned.

[54]Balazs, p. 40.

If an author were interested in developing the interior world of a character, the film would have some difficulty in portraying it. Hence, this limitation should be considered when evaluating the success of character adaptation.

SETTING

The physical locale against which the plot is developed and the characters operate is called setting. Its function is three-fold in that it partly controls the characters, suggests the theme (idea expressed by the work), and produces an atmosphere. Since setting is governed by plot, at least in part, it is an effective way to control our responses to the action. As plot is an artful selection of incidents, setting is an artful selection of the physical environment in which the plot takes place. However, while the writer is able to select elements within a particular scene to reinforce character, theme, and atmosphere and still produce a feeling of verisimilitude, the film customarily reproduces the realistic physicality of the scene, but much of the artful selection made by the writer is sometimes left to the audience. The problem here is found in a conflict of conventions. Realistic prose works do not operate like realistic films in this respect. On the other hand, expressionistic settings in fiction, that is, settings expressive of a character's inner state or attitude, can be duplicated in film. Thus, the director's most difficult task is to attempt to reproduce a selective but realistic locale without producing an expressionistic setting.

POINT OF VIEW

The plot of a prose work is mainly narrated from the point of view of an unidentified speaker outside the story or from the point of view of a character within the story. The outside narrator is either omniscient, one who has a total knowledge of the facts and can narrate this information either from the outside or inside of the particular characters to be found in any time and any place, or limited, one who is only privy to the facts known by one character in the story. In either case, the plot is narrated in the third person. If the story is told from the point of view of a character within the story itself, the reader is not only limited to the knowledge that the particular character is privy to, but the narrative is recounted in the actual words of that character. Such a point of view is called first-person narration.

On occasion, writers as diverse as Isherwood, Mann, and Robbe-Grillet have employed a "camera" point of view in which the material is presented in a totally objective manner exactly as a camera would record a situation. Also, while short stories tend to be presented from one point of view throughout, some novels, such as Joyce's *Ulysses*, mix first-person and third-person points of view. Since the writer is free to select a particular point of view or even a particular combination of points of view for a given story, such a selection becomes an important element in the art of the work. Many works have been weakened by a poor selection of point of view.

Film does not have the luxury of succeeding with as many points of view. It follows, then, that the quality of some literary works is not accessible to film. With care, an acceptable third-person-limited film can be made, but film customarily is narrated from a third-person-omniscient point of view. In such cases, the camera shifts back and forth from the role of detached observer (objective) to the point of view of one of the participants (subjective). Total "camera" films or totally subjective films are seldom successful, particularly as features, due to the monotony of the approaches. Although a number of films have been adapted from novels and short stories narrated in the first-person, such works almost always rely upon a convention that attempts to be analogous. The film may begin with a voice-over-visual narration to indicate the first person. Soon, the narration stops and the film gets told from the customary third-person point of view. From time to time, the narrator's voice recurs, reminding us of the first-person narration. It can be seen that such a technique is simply a film convention used to suggest the narrator's voice, but it scarcely can indicate the richness in a successful literary work resulting from the continual voice of the narrator telling the story. Some attempts have been made to make films with a first-person point of view throughout. In these instances the director comes into conflict with one of the main differences between prose and film—film best expresses itself visually. Film theorists have noted that when a voice and an image are of equal strength and are in competition for the viewer's attention, the image dominates. Hence, a film emphasizing verbal narration tends to weaken the visuals in order to make its point. Thus, first-person narrations can be achieved, but the outcome is seldom cinematically satisfactory in the fiction film.

STYLE

In literature, style may be defined as the writer's characteristic use of diction (word choice), grammar and syntax (the way words are arranged in sentences), and figures of speech (hyperbole, metaphor, personification, etc.). For example, Hemingway tends to use a sparse vocabulary, uncomplicated sentence construction, and few figures of speech. On the other hand, Faulkner's vocabulary is quite wide and learned, his sentences are often very complex, and he uses many figures of speech. Obviously, such distinctions are relative. Hemingway's diction is hardly inadequate for his purposes, but with respect to Faulkner's diction, it is sparse. Content influences such stylistic choices in the sense that all fictional elements should serve to reinforce the idea of the work. With this in mind, some readers look upon content, the worlds, situations, and ideas generally expressed by a particular writer, as an important influence upon his style.

V. I. Pudovkin, Eisenstein's colleague, was one of the first theoreticians to note that the shot, the photographed view of the subject, can be considered equal to the word in literature.[55] However, while the ability of film to reproduce concrete words ("bread," for example) is unlimited, cinematic reproduction of abstract words (for

[55]V. I. Pudovkin, "Introduction to the German Edition," *Film Technique and Film Acting*, ed. and trans. Ivor Montagu (New York: Grove Press, Inc., 1970), p. 24. "Introduction" first published in 1928. Most of the book was first published in Russia in 1926.

instance, "faith") is hindered by the same problems expressed in our earlier consideration of metaphor. Thus, if a director were to attempt to capture the diction of a particular work, it would be easier to adapt the concrete diction of Hemingway to the screen than the more abstract diction of Faulkner. For this reason, Hemingway's diction is more "cinematic" than Faulkner's. If a particular writer emphasizes abstract diction in order to produce an artful work, a successful adaptation will prove difficult.

As the word is equal to the shot, the combination of shots in a scene is equal to the sentence. Further, the various methods of transitions from scene to scene produce an effect similar to the paragraph and the chapter of a novel or section of a short story. The various methods of transition from shot to shot and from scene to scene suggest that editing is analogous to grammar, syntax, and paragraph construction in prose fiction. However, while film makes use of an analogous method, prose grammar, syntax, and construction are more precise. For example, while short duration shots often have the effect of sentences, one moving camera shot, in itself, might be a sentence or even a paragraph. Ernest Lindgren describes how the editing process works in film and we can see how this technique is analogous to grammar and syntax:

> The normal method of transition from shot to shot within a scene is by means of a cut which gives the effect of one shot being instantly replaced by the next. The normal method of transition from one scene to another is by means of the mix or dissolve which is always associated with a sense of the passage of time or a break in time. A sequence is normally punctuated by a fade-in at the beginning and a fade-out at the end. The fade may be quick or slow according to the emotional mood of the film at the moment it occurs and to the degree of emphasis which the director desires to give the pause at that particular point.[56]

While this is a description of traditional methods of editing, Lindgren's use of "normal" suggests that this is not always the case. Just as grammar and syntax are changing in modern literature, film

[56]Ernest Lindgren, *The Art of the Film* (New York: Macmillan, 1948), p. 67. Quoted in Bluestone, p. 18.

style in editing is changing also. For example, Bergman's *Persona* (1966) and Bunuel's *Belle De Jour* are almost entirely edited with cuts. Since both films are interested in the interior lives of their characters, rather than the exterior time of the plot, such editing is justified. When we consider the director's editing techniques employed in a filmic adaptation of literature, we should determine how well he uses the possibilities of editing to produce an analogy to the writer's grammar and syntax. Further, if the writer's constructions are traditional, the director should use traditional editing techniques; if the prose work is more experimental, the film should be edited accordingly. However, remember that film, by nature, is presented in the present tense.

The last stylistic element, figures of speech, may be thought of as language used connotatively or language used to express a departure from the literal meaning of the word. Irony, apostrophe, simile, metaphor, and symbol are representative figures of speech. Their use gives the writer a richer method of expression because he is able to describe through analogy or suggest connections in dissimilar things. As noted in the earlier treatment of metaphor, the film is limited in *visually* producing figures of speech. Thus, a writer making extensive use of this element of style would prove difficult to adapt to the screen.

Since the style of a great work of prose fiction is almost always integral to its aesthetic success, we are at the heart of the problem of cinematic adaptations. Film is not able to use analogous methods that satisfactorily reproduce a particular writer's style; hence those films that attempt stylistic adaptations are seldom successful. When they are, it will be found that the writer's style is analogous to the conventions of film style to begin with. However, this may not always be the case in future attempts. It should be remembered that film is an infant art and that it is capable of a much more accurate reproduction of literary style. The experiments in the uses of language by Godard (*One Plus One*, 1968) and the manipulation of time by Resnais (*Last Year at Marienbad*, 1961) suggest the possibilities. In *Literature and Film*, Robert Richardson makes a case for this view:

> The film language, which is the basis of film as a narrative art, seems still to be evolving, and it would be

premature and rash to suggest that it will not eventually develop language with the force, clarity, grace, and subtlety of written language.[57]

TONE

This is the most difficult device to identify in prose. While some suggest that tone is simply the author's attitude toward the material being presented as well as his attitude toward the audience, others choose to include mood, the atmosphere evoked by the material itself. Another way tone could be described would be to say that if theme is *what* a writer says through his work, tone is *how* he intones it. For our purposes, tone will be considered to be the writer's attitude toward the material and his audience (e.g., formal, informal, serious, playful, ironic, honest) as well as the mood or atmosphere found in the work. Tone may be expressed in many ways: diction and imagery are two major methods.

Diction used to present tone is obviously richer in language than in film. With imagery, it is another matter. While imagery has been considered synonymous with certain figures of speech, such as metaphor, simile, symbol, verbal appeals to our five senses are also thought of as imagery. Hence, while film is limited in its ability to adapt the writer's tone found in "visual" figures of speech, it is often able to produce sensory imagery to better effect than language. For instance, an actual sound in a film is more immediately perceived by an audience than onomatopoeia. Feelies, tasties, and smellies, thankfully, remain between the covers of science-fiction.

Tone expressed through mood is often more successful in films than in literature because literature presents its information linearly while film can convey various "messages" simultaneously. For example, a story may begin: "It was a cold, dark, rainy night . . ." and from time to time refer to properties of cold, darkness, and rain for reinforcement. On the other hand, a film could continually present darkness and rain visually, and coldness through certain

[57]Robert Richardson, *Literature and Film* (Bloomington, Ind.: Indiana University Press, 1969), p. 78.

actions of the actors and actresses. The visuals could be accompanied by realistic sounds of rain and appropriate mood music. Simultaneously, plot and action would continue. Thus, the film's analogous methods of producing literary mood are satisfactory and, often, more successful. The key to this success is the flexibility of film in its appeal to our senses. Sounds can be loud or soft, images can be under- or overexposed, the color of the film can be manipulated (even the color of black and white film), lenses can change the quality of the image, film stock of different speeds can be employed. The adapter's task is to select those visual and aural methods at his disposal that produce moods expressed in literature through language.

Rhythm, like diction and imagery, is not primarily a tonal device, but it is often employed in literature and film to that effect. While rhythm may be thought of as an element in poetry rather than prose, fiction is able to produce certain recurrences at regular intervals that either produce the tone of a particular passage or of the entire work. Prose rhythm is created through repetitions of words, recurrences of syntax patterns, and structurings of larger units such as paragraphs or sections. Once an artist sets up the basic tempo of the work, rhythmic changes may then be used as tone changes in given passages. The last paragraph of James Joyce's *The Dead* is a classic example of the use of prose rhythm for tonal effect. Here are the last two sentences of the paragraph:

> It [the snow] lay thickly drifted on the crooked crosses and headstones, on the spears of the little gate, on the barren thorns. His soul swooned slowly as he heard the snow falling faintly through the universe and faintly falling, like the descent of their last end, upon all the living and the dead.[58]

Rhythm in film is central to the concept of editing. Film rhythm may be divided into three types: interior, the quality of the movement within the shot; exterior, the length of time of each shot; and transitional, the length of time between the shots. As in prose, film

---

[58]James Joyce, *Dubliners*, first printing with corrected text by Robert Scholes (New York: Viking Press, Inc., 1967), pp. 223–224. Reprinted by permission of the publisher.

rhythm may be used to reinforce the material being presented, but it is also a fine method of producing tone.

Film rhythm has one advantage over prose rhythm; editing enables the director to manipulate time in a more immediate fashion than in prose. Interior action can be speeded up (shot at two frames/second) or slowed down (seventy frames/second); the exterior action may be punctuated with cuts, fades, or dissolves; likewise, transitions may be noted through cuts, fades, or dissolves. Since fades and dissolves may be made slowly or quickly, further flexibility results. The visual immediacy of film rhythm may often have a greater impact upon the audience than the methods of punctuation, syntax, or paragraph and section rhythm found in prose. Hence, when diction and imagery produce tone in a given work of prose, the director can sometimes create an analogous tone by placing a greater emphasis upon film rhythm.

THEME

As previously noted, theme is *what* the author or film-maker says about the subject or the plot. Since all serious prose fiction works have a theme, the film adaptation should attempt to reproduce it. Theme may be expressed through a combination of some or all of the fictional or cinematic elements previously mentioned. This is not to say that any given story or novel will present theme through a balanced use of the elements. Some works express theme through plot and character with stylistic and rhythmic elements used as reinforcements. Others may not be particularly concerned with plot and may, for example, emphasize character and tone to communicate the thematic point of the work. Thus, when evaluating a particular cinematic treatment of a novel or short story, assume that the most successful film adaptation will express the theme of the original work with a similar emphasis on those particular prose elements that the writer found most suitable.

Theme has been the downfall of many serious attempts at film adaptations of novels and short stories for three reasons. Martin C. Battestin notes them in his essay on *Tom Jones*:

> [The script writer's] vision is narrower than Fielding's:
> this is a function partly of the necessary limitations of
> scope in the film, partly of commercial pressures preclud-
> ing "moral seriousness" in a work designed to entertain
> millions, and partly of the different *Weltanshauung*
> [manner of looking at the world] of the twentieth
> century.[59]

Let us examine these reasons in order. The limitations of scope
in film will always be a problem. Naturally, analogy is very important here. If a literary theme is expressed through an elaborate
plot, a wealth of characters, and an elaborate use of figurative language, it would be senseless to call the film a failure because it
could not reproduce the complex theme of the original. However,
it might be possible that the director could carefully select representative parts of the plot, create fewer characters representing
traits, ideas, or positions of many, and substitute setting and tone
for figurative language. In this way, the film would be a successful
adaptation. The other two problems, commercial pressures and
manner of looking at the world, may not be as crucial in the future.
While well-produced film adaptations will always be as costly as
any film done well, the audience for such films is growing. Film
is fast becoming a medium capable of producing works of art as
well as vehicles of entertainment. While many have assumed this
for decades, some since the days of Griffith, we are presently seeing
an acceptance of this fact by the culture. Film as art is being taken
seriously by great masses in our culture and this, in turn, will en-
courage artful products. Such viewers will welcome works of "moral
seriousness" and they will also be able to consider other ways of
looking at the world, the world of the past as well as the present,
with the respect that such alternate views deserve. Naturally, there
will always be "entertainment" films, films made to wile away the
time and reinforce narrow preconceptions, but such shallow works
are to be found in any art form.

While literature and film are separate forms of art, the enter-
prising director will be able to produce an artful adaptation by
employing film techniques that are similar, but not equal to lit-

[59]Battestin, p. 45.

erary techniques. As previously mentioned, analogy is the key. The successful adaptation will not be a copy of the literary work, but a cinematic transformation that captures as much of the spirit and as many of the themes of the original as possible.

Julius Bellone has called the rise of film as an art form since World War II a "film renaissance."[60] This is surely the case, and considerations of film adaptations of literary works have an important place in this renaissance. Through a study of the relationships between literature and film, it is hoped that a knowledge of the similarities and differences between one of our oldest art forms and our youngest will be developed. The result of such an endeavor should be a clearer and more sophisticated understanding of both forms of art.

[60]Julius Bellone, ed., *Renaissance of the Film* (New York: Macmillan, 1970).

THE SHORT STORY

CONRAD AIKEN

Silent Snow,
Secret Snow

Just why it should have happened, or why it should have happened just when it did, he could not, of course, possibly have said; nor perhaps could it even have occurred to him to ask. The thing was above all a secret, something to be preciously concealed from Mother and Father; and to that very fact it owed an enormous part of its deliciousness. It was like a peculiarly beautiful trinket to be carried unmentioned in one's trouserpocket—a rare stamp, an old coin, a few tiny gold links found trodden out of shape on the path in the park, a pebble of carnelian, a sea shell distinguishable from all others by an unusual spot or stripe—and, as if it were any one of these, he carried around with him everywhere a warm and persistent and increasingly beautiful sense of possession. Nor was it only a sense of possession—it was also a sense of protection. It was as if, in some delightful way, his secret gave him a fortress, a wall behind which he could retreat into heavenly seclusion. This was almost the first thing he had noticed about it—apart from the oddness of the thing itself—and it was this that now again, for the fiftieth time, occurred to him, as he sat in the little schoolroom. It was the half hour for geography. Miss Buell was revolving with one finger, slowly, a huge terrestrial globe which had been placed on her desk. The green and yellow continents passed and repassed, questions were asked and answered, and now the little girl in front of him, Deirdre, who had a funny little constellation of freckles on the back of her neck, exactly like the Big Dipper, was standing up and telling Miss Buell that the equator was the line that ran round the middle.

Miss Buell's face, which was old and grayish and kindly, with gray stiff curls beside the cheeks, and eyes that swam very brightly, like little minnows, behind thick glasses, wrinkled itself into a complication of amusements.

"Ah! I see. The earth is wearing a belt, or a sash. Or someone drew a line around it!"

"Oh, no—not that—I mean—"

In the general laughter, he did not share, or only a very little. He was thinking about the Arctic and Antarctic regions, which of course, on the globe, were white. Miss Buell was now telling them about the tropics, the jungles, the steamy heat of equatorial swamps, where the birds and butterflies, and even the snakes, were like living jewels. As he listened to these things, he was already, with a pleasant sense of half-effort, putting his secret between himself and the words. Was it really an effort at all? For effort implied something voluntary, and perhaps even something one did not especially want; whereas this was distinctly pleasant, and came almost of its own accord. All he needed to do was to think of that morning, the first one, and then of all the others—

But it was all so absurdly simple! It had amounted to so little. It was nothing, just an idea—and just why it should have become so wonderful, so permanent, was a mystery—a very pleasant one, to be sure, but also, in an amusing way, foolish. However, without ceasing to listen to Miss Buell, who had now moved up to the north temperate zones, he deliberately invited his memory of the first morning. It was only a moment or two after he had waked up —or perhaps the moment itself. But was there, to be exact, an exact moment? Was one awake all at once? or was it gradual? Anyway, it was after he had stretched a lazy hand up towards the headrail, and yawned, and then relaxed again among his warm covers, all the more grateful on a December morning, that the thing had happened. Suddenly, for no reason, he had thought of the postman, he remembered the postman. Perhaps there was nothing so odd in that. After all, he heard the postman almost every morning in his life—his heavy boots could be heard clumping round the corner at the top of the little cobbled hill-street, and then, progressively nearer, progressively louder, the double knock at each door, the crossings and recrossings of the street, till finally the clumsy steps came stumbling across to the very door, and the tremendous knock came which shook the house itself.

(Miss Buell was saying "Vast wheat-growing areas in North America and Siberia."

Deirdre had for the moment placed her left hand across the back of her neck.)

But on this particular morning, the first morning, as he lay there with his eyes closed, he had for some reason *waited* for the post-man. He wanted to hear him come round the corner. And that was precisely the joke—he never did. He never came. He never had come—*round the corner*—again. For when at last the steps *were* heard, they had already, he was quite sure, come a little down the hill, to the first house; and even so, the steps were curiously different—they were softer, they had a new secrecy about them, they were muffled and indistinct; and while the rhythm of them was the same, it now said a new thing—it said peace, it said remoteness, it said cold, it said sleep. And he had understood the situation at once—nothing could have seemed simpler—there had been snow in the night, such as all winter he had been longing for; and it was this which had rendered the postman's first foot-steps inaudible, and the later ones faint. Of course! How lovely! And even now it must be snowing—it was going to be a snowy day—the long white ragged lines were drifting and sifting across the street, across the faces of the old houses, whispering and hushing, making little triangles of white in the corners between cobble-stones, seething a little when the wind blew them over the ground to a drifted corner; and so it would be all day, getting deeper and deeper and silenter and silenter.

(Miss Buell was saying "Land of perpetual snow.")

All this time, of course (while he lay in bed), he had kept his eyes closed, listening to the nearer progress of the postman, the muffled footsteps thumping and slipping on the snow-sheathed cobbles; and all the other sounds—the double knocks, a frosty far-off voice or two, a bell ringing thinly and softly as if under a sheet of ice—had the same slightly abstracted quality, as if removed by one degree from actuality—as if everything in the world had been insulated by snow. But when at last, pleased, he opened his eyes, and turned them towards the window, to see for himself this long-desired and now so clearly imagined miracle—what he saw instead was brilliant sunlight on a roof; and when, astonished, he jumped out of bed and stared down into the street, expecting to see the cobbles obliterated by the snow, he saw nothing but the bare bright cobbles themselves.

Queer, the effect this extraordinary surprise had had upon him—all the following morning he had kept with him a sense as of snow falling about him, a secret screen of new snow between himself and the world. If he had not dreamed such a thing—and how could he have dreamed it while awake?—how else could one explain it? In any case, the delusion had been so vivid as to affect his entire behavior. He could not now remember whether it was on the first or the second morning—or was it even the third?—that his mother had drawn attention to some oddness in his manner.

"But my darling—" she had said at the breakfast table—"what has come over you? You don't seem to be listening. . . ."

And how often that very thing had happened since!

(Miss Buell was now asking if anyone knew the difference between the North Pole and the Magnetic Pole. Deirdre was holding up her flickering brown hand, and he could see the four white dimples that marked the knuckles.)

Perhaps it hadn't been either the second or third morning—or even the fourth or fifth. How could he be sure? How could he be sure just when the delicious *progress* had become clear? Just when it had really *begun*? The intervals weren't very precise. . . . All he now knew was, that at some point or other—perhaps the second day, perhaps the sixth—he had noticed that the presence of the snow was a little more insistent, the sound of it clearer; and, conversely, the sound of the postman's footsteps more indistinct. Not only could he not hear the steps come round the corner, he could not even hear them at the first house. It was below the first house that he heard them; and then, a few days later, it was below the second house that he heard them; and a few days later again, below the third. Gradually, gradually, the snow was becoming heavier, the sound of its seething louder, the cobblestones more and more muffled. When he found, each morning, on going to the window, after the ritual of listening, that the roofs and cobbles were as bare as ever, it made no difference. This was, after all, only what he had expected. It was even what pleased him, what rewarded him: the thing was his own, belonged to no one else. No one else knew about it, not even his mother and father. There, outside, were the bare cobbles; and here, inside, was the snow. Snow growing heavier each day, muffling the world, hiding the ugly, and deadening increasingly—above all—the steps of the postman.

"But my darling—" she had said at the luncheon table—"what has come over you? You don't seem to listen when people speak to you. That's the third time I've asked you to pass your plate. . . ."

How was one to explain this to Mother? or to Father? There was, of course, nothing to be done about it: nothing. All one could do was to laugh embarrassedly, pretend to be a little ashamed, apologize, and take a sudden and somewhat disingenuous interest in what was being done or said. The cat had stayed out all night. He had a curious swelling on his left cheek—perhaps somebody had kicked him, or a stone had struck him. Mrs. Kempton was or was not coming to tea. The house was going to be house cleaned, or "turned out," on Wednesday instead of Friday. A new lamp was provided for his evening work—perhaps it was eye-strain which accounted for this new and so peculiar vagueness of his—Mother was looking at him with amusement as she said this, but with something else as well. A new lamp? A new lamp. Yes Mother, No Mother, Yes Mother. School is going very well. The geometry is very easy. The history is very dull. The geography is very interesting—particularly when it takes one to the North Pole. Why the North Pole? Oh, well, it would be fun to be an explorer. Another Peary or Scott or Shackleton. And then abruptly he found his interest in the talk at an end, stared at the pudding on his plate, listened, waited, and began once more—ah how heavenly, too, the first beginnings—to hear or feel—for could he actually hear it?— the silent snow, the secret snow.

(Miss Buell was telling them about the search for the Northwest Passage, about Hendrik Hudson, the Half Moon.)

This had been, indeed, the only distressing feature of the new experience: the fact that it so increasingly had brought him into a kind of mute misunderstanding, or even conflict, with his father and mother. It was as if he were trying to lead a double life. On the one hand he had to be Paul Hasleman, and keep up the appearance of being that person—dress, wash, and answer intelligently when spoken to—; on the other, he had to explore this new world which had been opened to him. Nor could there be the slightest doubt—not the slightest—that the new world was the profounder and more wonderful of the two. It was irresistible. It was miraculous. Its beauty was simply beyond anything—beyond speech as beyond thought—utterly incommunicable. But how then, between the two worlds, of which he was thus constantly aware, was he to keep a balance? One must get up, one must go to breakfast, one must talk with Mother, go to school, do one's lessons—and, in all this, try not to appear too much of a fool. But if all the while one was also trying to extract the full deliciousness of another and quite separate existence, one which could not easily (if at all) be spoken of—how was one to manage? How was one to explain? Would it be safe to explain? Would it be absurd? Would it merely mean that he would get into some obscure kind of trouble?

These thoughts came and went, came and went, as softly and secretly as the snow; they were not precisely a disturbance, perhaps they were even a pleasure; he liked to have them; their presence was something almost palpable, something he could stroke with his hand, without closing his eyes, and without ceasing to see Miss Buell and the schoolroom and the globe and the freckles on Deirdre's neck; nevertheless he did in a sense cease to see, or to see the obvious external world, and substituted for this vision the vision of snow, the sound of snow, and the slow, almost soundless, approach of the postman. Yesterday, it had been only at the sixth house that the postman had become audible; the snow was much deeper now, it was falling more swiftly and heavily, the sound of its seething was more distinct, more soothing, more persistent. And this morning, it had been—as nearly as he could figure—just about the seventh house—perhaps only a step or two above: at most, he had heard two or three footsteps before the knock had sounded.... And with each such narrowing of the sphere, each nearer approach of the limit at which the postman was first audible, it was odd how sharply was increased the amount of illusion which had to be carried into the ordinary business of daily life. Each day, it was harder to get out of bed, to go to the window, to look out at the—as always—perfectly empty and snowless street. Each day it was more difficult to go through the perfunctory motions of greeting Mother and Father at breakfast, to reply to their questions, to put his books together and go to school. And at school, how extraordinarily hard to conduct with success simultaneously the public life and the life that was secret. There were times when he longed—positively ached—to tell everyone about it—to burst out with it—only to be checked almost at once by a far-off feeling as of some faint absurdity which was inherent in it—but was it absurd?—and more importantly by a sense of mysterious power in his very secrecy. Yes: it must be kept secret. That, more and more, became clear. At whatever cost to himself, whatever pain to others—

(Miss Buell looked straight at him, smiling, and said, "Perhaps we'll ask Paul. I'm sure Paul will come out of his daydream long enough to be able to tell us. Won't you, Paul." He rose slowly from his chair, resting one hand on the brightly varnished desk, and deliberately stared through the snow towards the blackboard. It was an effort, but it was amusing to make it. "Yes," he said slowly, "it was what we now call the Hudson River. This he thought to be the Northwest Passage. He was disappointed." He sat down again, and as he did so Deirdre half turned in her chair and gave him a shy smile, of approval and admiration.)

At whatever pain to others.

This part of it was very puzzling, very puzzling. Mother was very nice, and so was Father. Yes, that was all true enough. He wanted to be nice to them, to tell them everything—and yet, was it really wrong of him to want to have a secret place of his own?

At bedtime, the night before, Mother had said, "If this goes on, my lad, we'll have to see a doctor, we will! We can't have our boy—" But what was it she had said? "Live in another world?" "Live so far away?" The word "far" had been in it, he was sure, and then Mother had taken up a magazine again and laughed a little, but with an expression which wasn't mirthful. He had felt sorry for her. . . .

The bell rang for dismissal. The sound came to him through long curved parallels of falling snow. He saw Deirdre rise, and had himself risen almost as soon—but not quite as soon—as she.

II

On the walk homeward, which was timeless, it pleased him to see through the accompaniment, or counterpoint, of snow, the items of mere externality on his way. There were many kinds of bricks in the sidewalks, and laid in many kinds of pattern. The garden walls too were various, some of wooden palings, some of plaster, some of stone. Twigs of bushes leaned over the walls; the little hard green winter-buds of lilac, on gray stems, sheathed and fat; other branches very thin and fine and black and desiccated. Dirty sparrows huddled in the bushes, as dull in color as dead fruit left in leafless trees. A single starling creaked on a weather vane. In the gutter, beside a drain, was a scrap of torn and dirty newspaper, caught in a little delta of filth: the word ECZEMA appeared in large capitals, and below it was a letter from Mrs. Amelia D. Cravath, 2100 Pine Street, Fort Worth, Texas, to the effect that after being a sufferer for years she had been cured by Caley's Ointment. In the little delta, beside the fan-shaped and deeply runneled continent of brown mud, were lost twigs, descended from their parent trees, dead matches, a rusty horse-chestnut burr, a small concentration of sparkling gravel on the lip of the sewer, a fragment of eggshell, a streak of yellow sawdust which had been wet and was now dry and congealed, a brown pebble, and a broken feather. Further on was a cement sidewalk, ruled into geometrical parallelograms, with a brass inlay at one end commemorating the contractors who had laid it, and halfway across, an irregular and random series of dog-tracks, immortalized in synthetic stone. He knew these well, and always stepped on them; to cover the little hollows with his own foot had always been a queer pleasure; today he did it once more, but perfunctorily and detachedly, all the while thinking of something else. That was a dog, a long time ago, who had made a mistake and walked on the cement while it was still wet. He had probably wagged his tail, but that hadn't been recorded. Now, Paul Hasleman, aged twelve, on his way home from school, crossed the same river, which in the meantime had frozen into rock. Homeward through the snow, the snow falling in bright sunshine. Homeward?

Then came the gateway with the two posts surmounted by

egg-shaped stones which had been cunningly balanced on their ends, as if by Columbus, and mortared in the very act of balance: a source of perpetual wonder. On the brick wall just beyond, the letter H had been stenciled, presumably for some purpose. H? H.

The green hydrant, with a little green-painted chain attached to the brass screw-cap.

The elm tree, with the great gray wound in the bark, kidney-shaped, into which he always put his hand—to feel the cold but living wood. The injury, he had been sure, was due to the gnaw-ings of a tethered horse. But now it deserved only a passing palm, a merely tolerant eye. There were more important things. Miracles. Beyond the thoughts of trees, mere elms. Beyond the thoughts of sidewalks, mere stone, mere brick, mere cement. Beyond the thoughts even of his own shoes, which trod these sidewalks obedi-ently, bearing a burden—far above—of elaborate mystery. He watched them. They were not very well polished; he had neglected them, for a very good reason: they were one of the many parts of the increasing difficulty of the daily return to daily life, the morning struggle. To get up, having at last opened one's eyes, to go to the window, and discover no snow, to wash, to dress, to descend the curving stairs to breakfast—

At whatever pain to others, nevertheless, one must persevere in severance, since the incommunicability of the experience de-manded it. It was desirable of course to be kind to Mother and Father, especially as they seemed to be worried, but it was also desirable to be resolute. If they should decide—as appeared likely—to consult the doctor, Doctor Howells, and have Paul inspected, his heart listened to through a kind of dictaphone, his lungs, his stomach—well, that was all right. He would go through with it. He would give them answer for question, too—perhaps such answers as they hadn't expected? No. That would never do. For the secret world must, at all costs, be preserved.

The bird-house in the apple-tree was empty—it was the wrong time of year for wrens. The little round black door had lost its pleasure. The wrens were enjoying other houses, other nests, re-moter trees. But this too was a notion which he only vaguely and grazingly entertained—as if, for the moment, he merely touched an edge of it; there was something further on, which was already assuming a sharper importance; something which already teased at the corners of his eyes, teasing also at the corner of his mind. It was funny to think that he so wanted this, so awaited it—and yet found himself enjoying this momentary dalliance with the bird-house, as if for a quite deliberate postponement and enhancement of the approaching pleasure. He was aware of his delay, of his smiling and detached and now almost uncomprehending gaze at the little bird-house; he knew what he was going to look at next: it was his own little cobbled hill-street, his own house, the little river at the bottom of the hill, the grocer's shop with the cardboard man in the window—and now, thinking of all this, he turned his head, still smiling, and looking quickly right and left through the snow-laden sunlight.

And the mist of snow, as he had foreseen, was still on it—a ghost of snow falling in the bright sunlight, softly and steadily floating and turning and pausing, soundlessly meeting the snow that covered, as with a transparent mirage, the bare bright cobbles. He loved it—he stood still and loved it. Its beauty was paralyzing—beyond all words, all experience, all dream. No fairy-story he had ever read could be compared with it—none had ever given him this extraordinary combination of ethereal loveliness with a something else, unnameable, which was just faintly and deliciously terrifying. What was this thing? As he thought of it, he looked upward towards his own bedroom window, which was open—and it was as if he looked straight into the room and saw himself lying half awake in his bed. There he was—at this very instant he was still perhaps actually there—more truly there than standing here at the edge of the cobbled hill-street, with one hand lifted to shade his eyes against the snow-sun. Had he indeed ever left his room, in all this time? since that very first morning? Was the whole progress still being enacted there, was it still the same morning, and himself not yet wholly awake? And even now, had the postman not yet come round the corner? . . .

This idea amused him, and automatically, as he thought of it, he turned his head and looked towards the top of the hill. There was, of course, nothing there—nothing and no one. The street was empty and quiet. And all the more because of its emptiness it occurred to him to count the houses—a thing which, oddly enough, he hadn't before thought of doing. Of course, he had known there weren't many—many, that is, on his own side of the street, which were the ones that figured in the postman's progress —but nevertheless it came to him as something of a shock to find that there were precisely *six*, above his own house—his own house was the seventh.

Six!

Astonished, he looked at his own house—looked at the door, on which was the number thirteen—and then realized that the whole thing was exactly and logically and absurdly what he ought to have known. Just the same, the realization gave him abruptly, and even a little frighteningly, a sense of hurry. He was being hurried—he was being rushed. For—he knit his brows—he couldn't be mistaken —it was just above the *seventh* house, his *own* house, that the postman had first been audible this very morning. But in that case—in that case—did it mean that tomorrow he would hear nothing? The knock he had heard must have been the knock of their own door. Did it mean—and this was an idea which gave him a really extraordinary feeling of surprise—that he would never hear the postman again?—that tomorrow morning the postman would already have passed the house, in a snow by then so deep as to render his footsteps completely inaudible? That he would have made his approach down the snow-filled street so soundlessly, so secretly, that he, Paul Haselman, there lying in bed, would not have waked in time, or, waking, would have heard nothing?

But how could that be? Unless even the knocker should be muffled in the snow—frozen tight, perhaps? . . . But in that case—

A vague feeling of disappointment came over him; a vague sad-ness, as if he felt himself deprived of something which he had long looked forward to, something much prized. After all this, all this beautiful progress, the slow, delicious advance of the postman through the silent and secret snow, the knock creeping closer each day, and the footsteps nearer, the audible compass of the world thus daily narrowed, narrowed, narrowed, as the snow soothingly and beautifully encroached and deepened, after all this, was he to be defrauded of the one thing he had so wanted—to be able to count, as it were, the last two or three solemn footsteps, as they finally approached his own door? Was it all going to happen, at the end, so suddenly? or indeed, had it already happened? with no slow and subtle gradations of menace, in which he could luxuriate?

He gazed upward again, towards his own window which flashed in the sun: and this time almost with a feeling that it would be better if he were still in bed, in that room; for in that case this must still be the first morning, and there would be six more mornings to come—or, for that matter, seven or eight or nine—how could he be sure?—or even more.

III

After supper, the inquisition began. He stood before the doctor, under the lamp, and submitted silently to the usual thumpings and tappings.

"Now will you please say 'Ah!'?"

"Ah!"

"Now again please, if you don't mind."

"Ah."

"Say it slowly, and hold it if you can—"

"Ah-h-h-h-h-h—"

"Good."

How silly all this was. As if it had anything to do with his throat! Or his heart or lungs!

Relaxing his mouth, of which the corners, after all this absurd stretching, felt uncomfortable, he avoided the doctor's eyes, and stared towards the fireplace, past his mother's feet (in gray slippers) which projected from the green chair, and his father's feet (in brown slippers) which stood neatly side by side on the hearth rug.

"Hm. There is certainly nothing wrong there . . ."

He felt the doctor's eyes fixed upon him, and, as if merely to be polite, returned the look, with a feeling of justifiable evasiveness.

"Now, young man, tell me,—do you feel all right?"

"Yes, sir, quite all right."

"No headaches? no dizziness?"

"No, I don't think so."

"Let me see. Let's get a book, if you don't mind—yes, thank you, that will do splendidly—and now, Paul, if you'll just read it, holding it as you would normally hold it—"

He took the book and read:

"And another praise have I to tell for this the city our mother, the gift of a great god, a glory of the land most high; the might of horses, the might of young horses, the might of the sea. . . . For thou, son of Cronus, our lord Poseidon, hast throned herein this pride, since in these roads first thou didst show forth the curb that cures the rage of steeds. And the shapely oar, apt to men's hands, hath a wondrous speed on the brine, following the hundred-footed Nereids. . . . O land that art praised above all lands, now is it for thee to make those bright praises seen in deeds."

He stopped, tentatively, and lowered the heavy book.

"No—as I thought—there is certainly no superficial sign of eye-strain."

Silence thronged the room, and he was aware of the focused scrutiny of the three people who confronted him. . . .

"We could have his eyes examined—but I believe it is something else."

"What could it be?" This was his father's voice.

"It's only this curious absent-minded—" This was his mother's voice.

In the presence of the doctor, they both seemed irritatingly apologetic.

"I believe it is something else. Now Paul—I would like very much to ask you a question or two. You will answer them, won't you —you know I'm an old, old friend of yours, eh? That's right! . . ."

His back was thumped twice by the doctor's fat fist,—then the doctor was grinning at him with false amiability, while with one fingernail he was scratching the top button of his waistcoat. Beyond the doctor's shoulder was the fire, the fingers of flame making light prestidigitation against the sooty fireback, the soft sound of their random flutter the only sound.

"I would like to know—is there anything that worries you?"

The doctor was again smiling, his eyelids low against the little black pupils, in each of which was a tiny white bead of light. Why answer him? why answer him at all? "At whatever pain to others"

—but it was all a nuisance, this necessity for resistance, this necessity for attention: it was as if one had been stood up on a brilliantly lighted stage, under a great round blaze of spotlight; as if one were merely a trained seal, or a performing dog, or a fish, dipped out of an aquarium and held up by the tail. It would serve them right if he were merely to bark or growl. And meanwhile, to miss these last few precious hours, these hours of which every minute was more beautiful than the last, more menacing—? He still looked, as if from a great distance, at the beads of light in the doctor's eyes, at the fixed false smile, and then, beyond, once more at his mother's slippers, his father's slippers, the soft flutter of the fire. Even here, even amongst these hostile presences, and in this arranged light, he could see the snow, he could hear it—it was in the corners of the room, where the shadow was deepest, under the sofa, behind the half-opened door which led to the dining room. It was gentler here, softer, its seethe the quietest of whispers, as if, in deference to a drawing room, it had quite deliberately put on its "manners"; it kept itself out of sight, obliterated itself, but distinctly with an air of saying, "Ah, but just wait! Wait till we are alone together! Then I will begin to tell you something new! Something white! something cold! something sleepy! something of cease, and peace, and the long bright curve of space! Tell them to go away. Banish them. Refuse to speak. Leave them, go upstairs to your room, turn out the light and get into bed—I will go with you, I will be waiting for you, I will tell you a better story than Little Kay of the Skates, or The Snow Ghost—I will surround your bed, I will close the windows, pile a deep drift against the door, so that none will ever again be able to enter. Speak to them! . . ." It seemed as if the little hissing voice came from a slow white spiral of falling flakes in the corner by the front window—but he could not be sure. He felt himself smiling, then, and said to the doctor, but without looking at him, looking beyond him still—

"Oh, no, I think not—"

"But are you sure, my boy?"

His father's voice came softly and coldly then—the familiar voice of silken warning. . . .

"You needn't answer at once, Paul—remember we're trying to help you—think it over and be quite sure, won't you?"

He felt himself smiling again, at the notion of being quite sure. What a joke! As if he weren't so sure that reassurance was no longer necessary, and all this cross-examination a ridiculous farce, a grotesque parody! What could they know about it? These gross intelligences, these humdrum minds so bound to the usual, the ordinary? Impossible to tell them about it! Why, even now, even now, with the proof so abundant, so formidable, so imminent, so appallingly present here in this very room, could they believe it?— could even his mother believe it? No—it was only too plain that if anything were said about it, the merest hint given, they would be incredulous—they would laugh—they would say "Absurd!"— think things about him which weren't true. . . .

"Why, no, I'm not worried—why should I be?"

He looked then straight at the doctor's low-lidded eyes, looked from one of them to the other, from one bead of light to the other, and gave a little laugh.

The doctor seemed to be disconcerted by this. He drew back in his chair, resting a fat white hand on either knee. The smile faded slowly from his face.

"Well, Paul!" he said, and paused gravely, "I'm afraid you don't take this quite seriously enough. I think you perhaps don't quite realize—don't quite realize—" He took a deep quick breath, and turned, as if helplessly, at a loss for words, to the others. But Mother and Father were both silent—no help was forthcoming.

"You must surely know, be aware, that you have not been quite yourself, of late? don't you know that? . . ."

It was amusing to watch the doctor's renewed attempt at a smile, a queer disorganized look, as of confidential embarrassment.

"I feel all right sir," he said, and again gave the little laugh.

"And we're trying to help you." The doctor's tone sharpened.

"Yes, sir, I know. But why? I'm all right. I'm just *thinking*, that's all."

His mother made a quick movement forward, resting a hand on the back of the doctor's chair.

"Thinking?" she said. "But my dear, about what?"

This was a direct challenge—and would have to be directly met. But before he met it, he looked again into the corner by the door, as if for reassurance. He smiled again at what he saw, at what he heard. The little spiral was still there, still softly whirling, like the ghost of a white kitten chasing the ghost of a white tail, and making as it did so the faintest of whispers. It was all right! If only he could remain firm, everything was going to be all right.

"Oh, about anything, about nothing,—you know the way you do!"

"You mean—day-dreaming?"

"Oh, no—thinking!"

"But thinking about *what*?"

"Anything."

He laughed a third time—but this time, happening to glance upward towards his mother's face, he was appalled at the effect his laughter seemed to have upon her. Her mouth had opened in an expression of horror. . . . This was too bad! Unfortunate! He had known it would cause pain, of course—but he hadn't expected it to be quite so bad as this. Perhaps—perhaps if he just gave them a tiny gleaming hint—?

"About the snow," he said.

"What on earth!" This was his father's voice. The brown slippers came a step nearer on the hearth rug.

"But my dear, what do you mean?" This was his mother's voice. The doctor merely stared.

"Just *snow*, that's all. I like to think about it."

"Tell us about it my boy."

"But that's all it is. There's nothing to tell. You know what snow is?"

This he said almost angrily, for he felt that they were trying to corner him. He turned sideways so as no longer to face the doctor, and the better to see the inch of blackness between the window-sill and the lowered curtain,—the cold inch of beckoning and delicious night. At once he felt better, more assured.

"Mother—can I go to bed, now, please? I've got a headache."

"But I thought you said—"

"It's just come. It's all these questions—! Can I, Mother?"

"You can go as soon as the doctor has finished."

"Don't you think this thing ought to be gone into thoroughly, and *now*?" This was Father's voice. The brown slippers again came a step nearer, the voice was the well-known "punishment" voice, resonant and cruel.

"Oh, what's the use, Norman—"

Quite suddenly, everyone was silent. And without precisely facing them, nevertheless he was aware that all three of them were watching him with extraordinary intensity—staring hard at him—as if he had done something monstrous, or was himself some kind of monster. He could hear the soft irregular flutter of the flames; the cluck-click-cluck-click of the clock; far and faint, two sudden spurts of laughter from the kitchen, as quickly cut off as begun; a murmur of water in the pipes; and then, the silence seemed to deepen, to spread out, to become worldlong and worldwide, to become timeless and shapeless, and to center inevitably and rightly, with a slow and sleepy but enormous concentration of all power, on the beginning of a new sound. What this new sound was going to be, he knew perfectly well. It might begin with a hiss, but it would end with a roar—there was no time to lose—he must escape. It mustn't happen here—

Without another word, he turned and ran up the stairs.

IV

Not a moment too soon. The darkness was coming in long white waves. A prolonged sibilance filled the night—a great seamless seethe of wild influence went abruptly across it—a cold low humming shook the windows. He shut the door and flung off his clothes in the dark. The bare black floor was like a little raft tossed in waves of snow, almost overwhelmed, washed under whitely, up again, smothered in curled billows of feather. The snow was laughing: it spoke from all sides at once: it pressed closer to him as he ran and jumped exulting into his bed.

"Listen to us!" it said. "Listen! We have come to tell you the story we told you about. You remember? Lie down. Shut your eyes, now—you will no longer see much—in this white darkness who could see, or want to see? We will take the place of everything. . . . Listen—"

A beautiful varying dance of snow began at the front of the room, came forward and then retreated, flattened out towards the floor, then rose fountain-like to the ceiling, swayed, recruited itself from a new stream of flakes which poured laughing in through the humming window, advanced again, lifted long white arms. It said peace, it said remoteness, it said cold—it said—

But then a gash of horrible light fell brutally across the room from the opening door—the snow drew back hissing—something alien had come into the room—something hostile. This thing rushed at him, clutched at him, shook him—and he was not merely horrified, he was filled with such a loathing as he had never known. What was this? this cruel disturbance? this act of anger and hate? It was as if he had to reach up a hand towards another world for any understanding of it,—an effort of which he was only barely capable. But of that other world he still remembered just enough to know the exorcising words. They tore themselves from his other life suddenly—

"Mother! Mother! Go away! I hate you!"

And with that effort, everything was solved, everything became all right: the seamless hiss advanced once more, the long white wavering lines rose and fell like enormous whispering sea-waves, the whisper becoming louder, the laughter more numerous.

"Listen!" it said. "We'll tell you the last, the most beautiful and secret story—shut your eyes—it is a very small story—a story that gets smaller and smaller—it comes inward instead of opening like a flower—it is a flower becoming a seed—a little cold seed—do you hear? we are leaning closer to you—"

The hiss was now becoming a roar—the whole world was a vast moving screen of snow—but even now it said peace, it said remoteness, it said cold, it said sleep.

CRITICISM OF
THE SHORT STORY

REUEL DENNEY

From
Conrad Aiken

...Few fictional works by a modern poet are as well known as Aiken's "Silent Snow, Secret Snow." A tapping into the stream of consciousness of a boy who appears to be relapsing into isolation and death wish, it is one of the best of the short stories in which Aiken has demonstrated his skill. Admiring Chekhov, James, and Andreyev, Aiken has worked mostly in the twentieth-century form of psychological fiction that we associate with Edouard Dujardin, Joyce, Dorothy Richardson, and Virginia Woolf. We should take special notice of Aiken's ability to repossess from the writers of fiction some of the tools they borrowed so readily from poets. The question of the relation between the poetry and the prose of Aiken might seem to be satisfied by referring to the blend of the symbolic and the psychological that we find in both. This reminiscence of the ambidextrous Poe is reinforced not by any interest of Aiken's in shrewd plotting but by his general attraction to the macabre and by the pleasure he sometimes takes in poetic texture as a resource of prose. Yet while most of Aiken's short stories offer complexity of character rather than plot they are not eventless. They ground themselves in those slowly gathering expectations that create suspense, provide the basis for dramatic reversal in the condition of the characters, and qualify the pieces as stories rather than portraits. /14/ . . .

Reuel Denney, *Conrad Aiken*, University of Minnesota Pamphlets on American Writers Number 38. University of Minnesota Press, Minneapolis. © Copyright 1964 University of Minnesota.

DISCUSSION QUESTION

What examples or evidence do you see of a blending of "the symbolic and the psychological" in the story?

DONALD HEINEY

From

Recent American Literature

... "Silent Snow, Secret Snow" is a fantasy of a child's dream-world, a sensitive study of the transition from childish daydreaming to neurosis. The small boy Paul Hasleman abandons himself to reveries of falling snow (he evidently lives in the South, and thus to him snow is wholly a thing of the imagination) and derives a secret pleasure from fancying the sound of the approaching footsteps of the postman in the silent whiteness. Withdrawing into his dreams, he gradually loses contact with his teacher, his parents, even the doctor who is called in to treat him. When his impatient father grows angry, Paul regresses completely into the dream world, aware of nothing but the insistence of the falling snow. The postman in this story is evidently a personification of death, and the snow fantasy itself a death-wish. /515/ ...

DISCUSSION QUESTIONS

1. Heiney suggests that Paul lives in the South and concludes that the snow is thus "wholly a thing of the imagination." What clues to setting do you find in the story? How is the somewhat unlocalized setting juxtaposed to the emphasis on geography?

Reprinted from *Recent American Literature* (Woodbury, N.Y.: Barron's Educational Series, Inc., 1958) by permission of the publisher.

2. What evidence do you find of the postman being a personification of death? How is the postman related to the final scene?

CLIFTON FADIMAN

From

Reading I've Liked

Much pink-edged nonsense has been written by moony adults about the child's "dream world." Few of us actually remember our childhood visions. But how willing most of us are to think up the kind of visions it would be pleasant to remember having had! Such reconstructions are generally mere compliments paid to the imaginative, poetical children we would so like to have been. It would be a sad thing for sentiment if it were known how many of us pass through childhood in a vacant daze, minds half closed and mouths half open.

But not all. A certain number of children create intense imaginary worlds for themselves, worlds far superior in interest to anything reality has to offer. They do not tell us about this world, except by vague hints, for communication breaks the spell. Undersympathetic adults call these vague hints lies. Oversympathetic adults call them genius. Both kinds of adults are wrong.

The child generally "outgrows," as we say, his fantasies. "Outgrows" may be a poor word, for sometimes the fantasy is the largest thing the child will ever know during his entire life. Adjustment to reality is not always a process of development; it may involve diminution. The man who lives and dies a slave may have had his largest and most liberated moments during a brief period of childhood reverie.

But the fantasy may never be outgrown. It may become necessary to the child, a permanent door of escape from the outer world. It may, as in the Conrad Aiken story that follows, "take the place of everything." Then it assumes the form of hallucination; a compulsion neurosis is born; and mental derangement, temporary or permanent, may result. This is the situation treated in "Silent Snow, Secret Snow," one of the most haunting tales in our literature.

Note how unclinical it is, though it could never have been written before the birth of psychiatry or even, I should judge, before the advent of psychoanalysis. On the other hand, it is not oversimplified. /734/ It is told not in the language of the twelve-year-old boy of the story but in that of a perceptive adult.

What makes "Silent Snow, Secret Snow" a masterly piece of writing is not that it is a successful study of the mechanism by which a mind fatally splits itself. The value of the tale lies in its human sympathy. Each of us has a secret place of his own into which, like a wounded animal, he crawls when things get too much for him. Paul Hasleman's place, his "secret screen of new snow between himself and the world," is merely our own private evasion magnified and intensified. Paul is not only a mental case. He is, so wise and true is this story, part of ourselves./735/

DISCUSSION QUESTION

Fadiman suggests that the fantasy is "a permanent door of escape from the outer world." What in the outer world is Paul trying to flee?

FREDERICK HOFFMAN

From
Conrad Aiken

... The most famous of Aiken's child sensibilities is the hero of "Silent Snow, Secret Snow." This story begins, as does "Strange Moonlight," with a mystery partly invented, at least willfully encouraged and prolonged. The great difference is that in "Silent Snow, Secret Snow" it is never allowed to "break" against the facts. "It was as if, in some delightful way, his secret gave him a fortress, a wall behind which he could retreat into heavenly seclusions." ... In school, while Miss Buell tells him and his fellow students about the tropics, he remains within the cold securities of the Arctic and Antarctic. Night after night the vision of the secret snow increases; he wills that it shut off all human sounds, and he measures each morning how remote it makes the sound of the postman's steps, "... as if removed by one degree from actuality—as if everything had been insulated by snow." ... It pleased him that there should be no actual snowfall, that the snow should remain secret—his own willed conceit hiding the ugly world.

Inevitably the separation brings him into a clash with his parents. How keep a balance between the two worlds? It was becoming increasingly difficult to make the leap from one into the other; it was easier and more tempting to remain in the world of his own imagining. "At whatever pain to others, nevertheless, one must persevere in severance, since the incommunicability of the experience demanded it ..."

Finally the "severance" is complete. He breaks angrily from his parents and the doctor, who are trying to intrude into his mystery;

Reprinted with permission of Twayne Publishers, Inc. from *Conrad Aiken* (New York, 1962), pp. 40–41.

and, as he re-enters his room, "a cold low humming shook the windows." The snow enters his room; it is suddenly, terribly disturbed by a "gash of horrible light," his mother's opening the door, which forces it to draw back, hissing. Turning to his mother, he shouts to her to go away—he hates her. And, with that, the matter is settled.

> ... everything was solved, everything became all right: the seamless hiss advanced once more, the long white wavering lines rose and fell like enormous whispering sea-waves, the whisper becoming louder, the laughter more numerous.

> —the whole world was a vast moving screen of snow— but even /40/ now it said peace, it said remoteness, it said sleep.

This story is the most sensational, as it is the most memorable, of those about Aiken's "lost people." The narrative consistently stays within the boy's mind, moving with it toward his destruction, never suggesting or stating reasons or trying to probe "psychologically" into the boy's injured spirit. It is a psychic scene of remarkable purity; the adult world stays always dimly at the fringe of the boy's awareness and of his sense of his relationship. What has caused the aberration is never revealed, but his desire to withdraw from human communication is faithfully followed to its ultimate, total rejection of the family and submission to the vision. The snow is death, or the means to death, a confrontation of infinity or of natural immensities. /41/ ...

DISCUSSION QUESTIONS

1. Hoffman mentions the "balance between two worlds." How does Aiken describe Paul's balancing act? What finally destroys the balance?
2. Hoffman believes that the snow is death. What qualities of the snow suggest death?

EDWARD STONE

From
Voices of Despair

. . . In "Silent Snow, Secret Snow" what gives Aiken's
screw an extra turn is that the horror befalls a child, a boy whose
mind finally breaks down, gradually but inexorably overpowered by
a silent and secret substance that is a continuous snowfall. From
nowhere it appears, muffling the ugly world of reality, at first from
a distance, then more closely and urgently, its beauty "this extraordinary combination of etheral loveliness with a something else,
unnameable, which was just faintly and deliciously terrifying.
What was this thing?" If we consider that this thing was the
destruction of a human's mind, then it was death. And even a
personified death, as the child's mind would imagine it with terrifying vividness, a death that completely separates its victim from
his schoolmates, his father and mother, and leaves him in its
dubious safety and security from reality—enveloped by its warmth
/126/ but buried in its depths. Rightly the fairy-tale element is
prominent, for that is the version of life and death whose terrible
reality curdles children's blood. "No fairy story he had ever read
could be compared with it," Paul Hasleman thinks of this silent,
secret substance; and it whispers to him that, if he will forsake all
others, it will reward him with "a better story than Little Kay of
the Skates, or The Snow Ghost—I will surround your bed, I will
close the windows, pile a deep drift against the door, so that none
will ever again be able to enter." Bewitched by the insidious and
hypnotic whiteness, he never struggles against it; and where the

Reprinted from *Voices of Despair: Four Motifs in American Literature* (Athens, 1966) by permission of the Ohio University
Press.

man in Frost's "Stopping By Woods" can shake off the inviting darkness by reminding himself of responsibilities, Aiken's boy sits by helplessly and is enveloped by the fatal whiteness. Placed beside this story, Hans Christian Andersen's horrors can seem subdued. If frivolous Karen loses her feet in her passion for the bewitched red shoes, eventually her repenting soul flies up to heaven; at length she is welcomed by the angel of God in white garments, by organ song and children's choir. Paul's death is the more painful for its freedom from physical pain; the afterlife that waits for him, the more appalling for its utter separation from human voices./127/...

DISCUSSION QUESTION

Stone calls attention to the "fairy-tale element" in the story. What elements of the fairy tale do you find in the story?

RALPH H. SINGLETON

"Silent Snow,
Secret Snow"

It was when he was an undergraduate at Harvard University that Conrad Aiken first developed an absorbing interest in Havelock Ellis, Sigmund Freud, and other psychologists. More and more he became fascinated by the study of abnormal psychology, mental aberrations of one kind or another, schizophrenia— that psychosis described by the *New World Dictionary* as "a mental disorder characterized by indifference, withdrawal, hallucinations, and delusions of persecution and omnipotence, often with unimpaired intelligence."

"Silent Snow, Secret Snow" describes the developing psychosis in a twelve-year-old boy, a tour de force, depicting what is going on in the boy's mind. All of the symptoms mentioned in the definition above can be observed in Paul. The increasing separation /10/ from his environment, with the forcing himself back to it becoming increasingly difficult, is typified by the muffled and more muffled steps of the postman, gradually fading out of hearing as the other world, a delicious world of swirling snow, approaches. He had been fascinated by the thought of snow mentioned by Miss Buell, his teacher, in the frigid zones of the north, "land of perpetual snow,"

From Ralph H. Singleton, *Instructor's Manual to Two and Twenty: A Collection of Short Stories* (New York, 1962). Re printed by permission of St. Martin's Press, Inc.

as she discussed geography in class; and he had been waiting eagerly for the lovely white snow to fall upon the streets and sidewalks and houses with the approach of winter. His sense of persecution increases—from his parents, from the doctor—until it reaches the pitch of his shouted exclamation: "Mother! mother! Go away! I hate you!" His feeling of omnipotence grows pronounced. His smile is a smile of superiority, as the doctor badgers him to tell if there is anything that worries him. "They" simply won't be able to understand. In school he is amused by the commonplace quality of the classroom. He feels a "sense of mysterious power," which lifts him above those around him. His mother and father must be pacified—but it is distressing to have to make the effort. What he wants to do is to "explore this new world which has been opened to him," and the new world is "the profounder and more wonderful of the two."

We get an occasional look at Paul from the outside through his comments about his teacher, his mother and father, the doctor. His parents notice his increased absorption in this dream world. "You don't seem to listen when people speak to you," his mother says. "I'm sure Paul will come out of his daydream long enough to be able to tell us. Won't you Paul?" says his teacher, smiling at him. Paul is aware of the two worlds at the same time. He hears every word of Miss Buell, his teacher, as his mind reverts to his recollection of the approach of the postman through the snow, and he stares "through the snow toward the blackboard" as he answers her question. His mother and father seem "to be worried" about him. And when he is finally examined by the doctor and laughs at their attempts to pin him down to something, he sees his mother looking at him, her mouth opened "in an expression of horror."

The selection of snow as a blanketing medium, shutting out the world of his environment, is a happy choice, as is the device of the postman's feet becoming increasingly muffled, the sound of his approach being delayed more and more until the secret world of his own has blotted out reality by his complete withdrawal. We are, of course, entirely within the mind of the boy from the first words in the story until the last, when, since that mind is shutting itself off from reality, we are also shut off with it. /11/

DISCUSSION QUESTION

Singleton notes that readers are "entirely within the mind of the boy" from the first of the story to the last. Aiken uses third-person-limited point of view. What would be gained or lost if the story were told from the first-person point of view?

LEO HAMALIAN

Aiken's "Silent Snow, Secret Snow"

Since "Silent Snow, Secret Snow" is not a clinical case history [Exp., June, 1947, v, Q25], but on the contrary, a short story, fleeting and elusive in character, "rich in shimmering overtones of hint and suggestion," a definitive interpretation will seem specious and glib, for indeed Aiken, who may see and know all, doesn't tell all. However, he drops enough calico in his trail to show the direction he has taken.

Enigmatic Paul Hasleman may be losing: (1) his hearing, (2) his life, (3) his sanity, (4) his innocence. Theory one is insupportable, two possible but implausible literally, three exaggerated, and four incomplete, but elements of each contribute towards rewarding speculation.

First, Aiken, at the age of eleven, saw his father kill his mother and then commit suicide. The emotional impact of this tragic experience suggests a parallel if milder psychic disturbance in the life of Paul and renders as unlikely any overly simplified explanation, such as theory one. Second, Aiken's prose is psychological and shows the influence of Freud.

Fascinated by Freud's study of the mind, his own laid open by tragedy, Aiken may be delineating the veiled death-wish of an adolescent, much as Bryant did in *Thanatopsis*, or giving expression to Rank's "birth trauma" theory, which dimly recalls the Freudian death-wish. (Rank maintained that the shock of leaving the womb and entering an unfriendly world is the basic cause of emotional trouble; neurosis is a misguided attempt to return to the uterus, or to obtain rebirth.) In the final paragraph of "Snow," the key lines, "a story that gets small and smaller," etc., finds exquisite equation

Reprinted from *Explicator*, VII (1948), item 17, by permission of the author and *Explicator*, copyright holder.

in Aiken's *Preludes for Memnon*: "The snowflake was my father; I return After this interval of faith and question, To nature's heart, in pain, as I began." Paul moves from a hostile, insecure, ugly world to a pure, friendly, secure world (return to the womb), and in another vein, wishes that part of him in reality to die.

Paul shows preoccupation (a sign of anxiety) with his phantasy of the snow. Gradually withdrawing from the world of reality to that of phantasy, he still has a foot in each. Confronted simultaneously with the growing demands of puberty and the sudden revelation of sex, Paul fails to take either in stride. As Freud might say, the libido, instead of projecting outward, turns in on the ego and inflates it much as a pump does a tire. As a modern psychoanalyst might say, Paul, to allay anxiety, mobilizes his resources and energies so as to insure the safety of his superior world and maintain himself as a separate entity. Obviously, he dreads blunderers, such as the doctor and his parents, that threaten his independence and self-sufficiency. Preoccupied with his own world, Paul does not make friends. Beleaguered by his parents, he worries and retreats. Therefore, Paul, apparently inactive, is actually fatigued by the effort involved in living a split existence. These symptoms are strongly reminiscent of clinical histories of neurasthenia, or a withdrawal neurosis. (Neurasthenia was the term common at the time "Snow" first appeared.)

The cause of the neurosis is implicit rather than explicit, and determination of it depends upon acceptance of these Freudian principles: phantasies and dreams contain material that helps us to identify and understand repressed neurotic tendencies; phantasies involve censorship and distortion; the temporal repetition of an act is habitually represented in dreams or phantasies by the numerical multiplication of an object.

In tortured Freudian style, Aiken hints at an Oedipal situation coming to a head. If we assume, then, that an early Oedipal fixation is remanifesting itself in Paul, we may account for the almost pathologically cold relationship between father and son. It seems possible that Paul has either interrupted his parents in the sexual act, or has become aware that they cohabit. Not only is his mother intimate with his father, whom Paul has already rejected, but she sides with him in the oral inquisition; therefore, Paul also rejects her and her world and withdraws further into his own.

The North Pole, the gateway post, the front of the house, the postman are clearly Freudian male symbols (the postman, who delivers the mail, becomes the male, through distortion); the window, the door, the room, the house, the bird-house, the hydrant, female. The post with the two stones cemented on top catches Paul's attention during his homeward hike. He thrusts his arm into the hole in the elm tree; he associates the North Pole with the Big Dipper; he waits for the postman to approach the house.

The carpet of snow may be a censored recollection of bed sheets, and Aiken has already told us what the snowflakes represent. The sound of the "ugly" footsteps becomes gradually muffled as Paul unconsciously expresses revulsion to the thought of the "clumsy steps" that "came stumbling across to the very door." On the other hand, as the postman draws closer, Paul as yet cannot deny what he saw or interrupted. In one world, he rejects reality; in the other, he accepts it. Many neurotics hear their hallucinations. All of the pieces do not fall into place, but as Freud says, the significance of some phantasy fragments remains unknown.

DISCUSSION QUESTIONS

1. Hamalian ties Aiken's childhood experiences to the story. What kinds of dangers do you see in this kind of biographical criticism? What are its strengths?

2. What details in the story suggest an "Oedipal situation"? How legitimate are Hamalian's speculations about what Paul might have seen?

WILLIAM M. JONES

Aiken's "Silent Snow, Secret Snow"

In "Silent Snow, Secret Snow" Aiken reveals the final break with reality that comes in some forms of mental illness. Paul Hasleman is first seen on the morning of the day on which this break occurs. Aiken permits his reader to see only through the eyes of this greatly disturbed twelve-year-old. The boy's thoughts are first revealed at school, where he is simultaneously wishing for the all-engulfing snow that frequently shuts out the world and attempting to hold on to reality. He maintains a sort of hold by concentrating on the girl in front of him: "Deirdre, who had a funny little constellation of freckles on the back of her neck," "Deirdre had for the moment placed her left hand across the back of her neck." And the schoolroom scene concludes with the suggestion that Paul is dependent upon Deirdre's unknowing help in retaining his contact with the real world: "He saw Deirdre rise, and had himself risen almost as soon—but not quite as soon—as she."

Paul's careful study of Deirdre's freckles seems to be explained by what Carl Jung in The Psychology of Dementia Praecox (New York, 1936) calls "fascination," a "distraction to the environment in order to conceal the vacuum of inner associations or the complex producing the vacuum." When Paul was questioned later about his problems, "abruptly he found his interest in the talk at an end, stared at the pudding on his plate, listened, waited, and began once more—ah how heavenly, too, the first, beginning—to hear or feel ... the silent snow, the secret snow."

Paul, recalling the onset of his desire, reveals many of the characteristics of a schizoid personality. He is engaged in what William F. McAuley in The Concept of Schizophrenia (London, 1953)

Reprinted from Explicator, XVIII (1960), item 34, by permission of the author and Explicator, copyright holder.

calls "the repudiation of reality." The sound of the school bell seems to Paul "removed by one degree from actuality—as if everything in the world had been insulated by snow." The snow was "muffling the world, hiding the ugly. . . ." Paul wonders how to keep a balance in one world and yet feel "the full deliciousness of another and quite separate existence."

The second section of the story, Paul's walk home from school, shows these frantic attempts to hold on to reality and yet enjoy the other world as well. Over and over Aiken sets Paul's two worlds against each other. Paul sees in the gutter every detail of "a little delta of filth." He sees the tracks of a dog in the hardened cement but suddenly, at the word "wet," the cement becomes a river "frozen into rock. Homeward through the snow . . . ." And Paul is lost again from reality. The paragraph concludes with a doubtful "Homeward?" But Paul brings himself back again by observing carefully two posts and a letter H. These do not necessarily need to be viewed as Freudian symbols, as Leo Hamalian has suggested (EXP., Nov., 1948, vii, 17). Aiken, as artistically as possible, is simply showing Paul's wobbling: "on the brick wall just beyond the letter H had been stenciled, presumably for some purpose, H? H." The H shows the boy's wavering mind at work.

Near the conclusion of Paul's homeward walk he discovers that he will never again hear the postman, Aiken's very apt symbol for the bringer of information from the outside world. In the third section of the story Paul's final shout to his mother, "Go away! I hate you!" helps him sever his last emotional tie with the physical world. "And with that effort, everything was solved, everything became all right."

Within an artistically organized unit Aiken has presented with numerous specific details from his own psychological knowledge the complete disintegration of a personality. McAuley says, "In the development of the schizophrenic personality not only are these fundamental maturing processes arrested but they are already diminishing." Aiken's snow concludes: "We'll tell you the last . . . small story—a story that gets smaller and smaller—it comes inward instead of opening like a flower—it is a flower becoming a seed—a little cold seed."

DISCUSSION QUESTIONS

1. Jones states that Paul depends upon "Deirdre's unknowing help in retaining his contact with the real world." What in the story suggests that Deirdre is in fact a reference point? What does it suggest about Paul?

2. Do you agree that the postman is Aiken's symbol for the "bringer of information from the outside world?" How is his function comparable to the teacher's? The doctor's?

ANN LANDMAN

"Silent Snow, Secret Snow"
The Child as Artist

William M. Jones has recently analyzed Conrad Aiken's "Silent Snow, Secret Snow" as a study, done imaginatively and sympathetically, but almost clinically, of schizophrenia.[1] He interprets the isolation of the hero as a schizophrenic repudiation of reality that culminates in a catatonic trance. Such an explication, such an analysis of Paul Hasleman's case, reflects the laboratory wisdom—the laboratory knowledge, rather—of this world. Very probably, the doctor called in to examine the boy might have offered just such a diagnosis to the Haslemans if he had been privileged to read Paul's thoughts.

That such an intention was Aiken's, however, is considerably less demonstrable. It is the purpose of this paper to suggest another interpretation which also fits the facts that Aiken has given but which deals with a symbolic, not a clinical, reading of these facts.

Since the story is told from the point of view of Paul himself, without any explicit commentary from Aiken in the person of storyteller, Paul's vision must contain almost all the clues that Aiken intended to give us, with one exception to be mentioned later, and this technique compels us to create our own commentary upon the available clues. My thesis is that Paul's withdrawal is not psychopathic, but rather the alienation of the artist from society, and that the price of this creative *apartheid* is death. Such a theme

Reprinted with permission of the author and publisher from *Studies in Short Fiction*, I (1963), 123-128.

[1]Conrad Aiken's "Silent Snow, Secret Snow" is quoted from *The Collected Short Stories of Conrad Aiken* (New York, 1960). The psychological interpretation is offered by William M. Jones, *Explicator* XVIII (March, 1960), Item 34.

stems, of course, from the romantic movement and appears in much of the literature of the twentieth-century, e.g., in Willa Cather's "Paul's Case," in much of Kafka and Joyce and Yeats, and in Mann's *Tonio Kröger*, and it has been traced back to the theme of the artist's melancholia in Burton and in Dürer, through Coleridge, Baudelaire, and the French Symbolists. As Frank Kermode points out in *The Romantic Image*, to experience that " 'epiphany' which is the Joycean equivalent to Pater's vision," the artist has to suffer profoundly, risk his very soul, and be alone, "not only to be separate /123/ from all others, but to have not even one friend."[2] Such a price in isolation is the inevitable concomitant of the artist's perception of what Kermode calls "the Image as a radiant truth out of space and time."[3]

Aiken applies the term "counterpoint" to Paul's two kinds of vision: his strange perception of the snow and his recognition of a pattern of visible details of the world of phenomena. Jones says of even the quaint observation of Deirdre's freckles, which formed the pattern of the Big Dipper, that it is a manifestation of abnormal psychology; and he cites Carl Jung's account of "fascination" as a "distraction to the environment in order to conceal the vacuum of inner associations or the *complex* producing the vacuum."[4] Aside from the fact that Paul has a vision, not a vacuum, to depart from and that he does not welcome any departure, it would seem a highly dangerous reading of far too much into an innocent observation. Any poet who "numbers the streaks of the tulip," it seems, would be in danger of the same kind of analysis. One is reminded of the late Professor Irwin Edman's anecdote of the psychiatrist who offered to cure him of his philosophy. Even if Paul were a schizophrenic (a point of view which I palpably do not accept), he would still be a valid symbol of the alienated artist, and the diagnosis of madness would leave unanswered the larger question of an ethically mad or spiritually blind society, guilty of the organized, bizarre sanity that can be cured only through such humane figures as Giraudoux's Madwoman.

[2]Frank Kermode, *The Romantic Image* (New York, 1957), p. 2.
[3]Ibid.
[4]Jones is using Carl Jung, *The Psychology of Dementia Praecox* (New York, 1936).

What Aiken does with the details of Paul's awareness, though, seems less a study of psychological "fascination" than an application of Conrad's precept that the artist should make us *see* the visible universe, as well as share the artist's private, inner vision of what is enduring.

The entire story is, to use Aiken's term, a delicate counterpointing of two ways of considering reality: one, under the aspect of eternity, and the other, simply as phenomena are perceived, or as they might be perceived, by either a poet or a sharp-eyed, spontaneous child. The conflict in Paul between these two levels of vision, which finally become irreconcilable, culminates in a choice which he must make, and ultimately it results in his death.

The vision which manifests itself through the symbolism of the snow is at first undemanding; it comes unsought as a precious /124/ mystery, conveying "a beautiful sense of possession." It carries with it a simple delight. Just so, the artist is always entranced initially with the beauty and charm of what Robert Graves calls the White Goddess; only later is he painfully enchanted, left alone and palely loitering. The snow is "just an idea," that is, a country of the mind which Paul may inhabit at the same time that he is counting Deirdre's freckles or contemplating the green and yellow continents of his geography class. Paul is abstracting "one degree from actuality" and naturally turns to images to express his miraculous vision, which is superior to "mere actuality."

Almost at once Paul's vision becomes a screen that covers with beauty the ugliness of the world of particulars, such as the little "deltas of filth" in the gutter. Aiken is by no means the first artist of our century to perceive the aesthetic discontinuity experienced by any serious lover of beauty in a world of "ambition, distraction, uglification, and derision." And as Paul's vision becomes more demanding, it imposes itself between the merely actual world and Paul. Hence he must lead a double life. His artistic integrity makes demands: he must be true to his vision "at whatever pain." His reward is that he may inhabit his unusual country of the mind. The proof of his controlling intellect is that he may inhabit his usual world as well whenever he needs to do so. The beauty is "beyond anything," pure, remote, and peaceful; but Paul is still sane and no fool as the world judges, even as the shrewd Miss

Buell judges. When she suspects him of the usual childish day-dreaming or failure to pay attention in class and challenges him, "I'm sure Paul will come out of his day-dream long enough to be able to tell us. Won't you, Paul?" he finds it amusing to make the required effort of attention immediately and answer her question about the Hudson River, however trivial it strikes him.

As the vision narrows and sharpens, "how sharply [is] increased the amount of illusion that [has] to be carried into the ordinary business of daily life," for the ideal is a cold transforming light upon the so-called real. Aiken here applies to the artist's vision terms that suggest a Platonic dichotomy between the absolute ideal forms and the multiple, various realm of "becoming."

Part of the pain which Paul must suffer results from the demand of secrecy that the vision imposes. Aiken's treatment of this portion of the story is meaningful in terms of the artist's conflict of loyalties and his need for creative solitude. It is álso (like Forster's "The Celestial Omnibus") an indictment of the hampering adults who would limit the sensitive child and deprive him of his right of /125/ privacy. The increased demand for secrecy is surely justified: "Was it wrong to want a secret place?" The vision becomes inexorable as Paul crosses the river homeward, and it ascends from mere things to images or thoughts of them and thence to eternity. Such an account accords well with the phenomenological progression with its "eidetic reduction," and it is also a kind of ascent up the Platonic ladder of beauty. Mortal limitations make the terrifying process partly incomprehensible to Paul.

For instance, Paul is not aware of the full implications of the developing crisis of family loyalties, though he has sensed that "at whatever pain" can mean pain to others as well as to himself. Nor does he think of the snow as akin to death, but merely akin to sleep. For the reader, though, who watches Paul pass almost insensibly through the degrees toward eternity, it is evident that Paul must reach this eternity ultimately only through dying.[5] There is a kind of dramatic irony in Paul's failure to perceive that the steps have finally reached his house. He does begin to wonder whether

[5] I am indebted to Mrs. J. S. Lewis for the suggestion, offered in conversation, that the postman is a surrogate for the Messenger or Angel of Death.

this means that he will never hear the postman again. Jones takes this figure merely to be "news from the outside world," but that is a conclusion of the two levels of reality, which have already been defined.

In the third division of the story, the world exacts its price from Paul. If the spiral of snow is inexorable, it is overbalanced by the cruel inquisition which is held. The parents, frightened by the calm and courteous quality of Paul's separateness as much as by, one suspects, the separation itself, call in a doctor. Paul can answer the doctor's questions, of course, and he also understands perfectly well what the doctor is assuming. Mrs. Hasleman is sympathetic, but Paul recognizes very soon his father's "punishment voice," which is inexorable and cruel. Paul himself sees that thè ordeal reduces him to the status of a performing dog (surely an indictment of the psychologists) and feels cruelly spotlighted as well. Aiken is not just giving us Paul's bias; he plainly offers objective facts and the emotionally charged glare of the investigation the way Paul experiences them; they ought to speak for themselves. It is damning evidence against a society of philistines that they would choose this method of limiting the artist, destroying him, or—worst of all— curing him.

If the inquisition does not plainly offer the clues for its own interpretation, there is yet another profoundly beautiful and ironic /126/ commentary upon Paul's ordeal: the passage which he reads aloud for the benefit of the Haslemans and the doctor. Its ostensible use is to test Paul's ability to hold a book correctly and read accurately the words on a printed page, and to everyone but Paul it is merely that. What it is to him—that is, what the passage means to him—he does not say, but it is his own choice: the choral ode at the heart of *Oedipus at Colonus*, the section praising the Grove of Athens, haunt sacred to love and the hospitable gods and the Muses—Athens, honored by the gods with the gifts of ships and horses that men might tame. The choral poem is the lyrical and symbolic statement of the meaning of the last play that Sophocles wrote, in which the reviled and banished Oedipus is at last granted a fair dismissal: first to be received magnanimously and compassionately by Theseus, then to find, though in darkness, a way into the mystic grove and a death that is rather an apotheosis. A reference to this choral poem, then, is a highly allusive way for the author to suggest an interpretation of all the facts of the story: a hero tragically isolated and wrongly condemned by society, the images of artistic control and understanding, and finally a vision of death and the transcendence of pain.

Aiken allows this Sophoclean passage to be read, but unsullied by any possible misunderstanding on the part of the parents or the doctor. They, instead, proceed to force Paul to some admission about his private vision. Under the pressure of these inquisitors Paul does reveal that his secret is "just thinking," and he comes as close as he dares to his image of the snow. He must not interpret it. It is possible that he could not have done so satisfactorily, for he is a child of twelve. What is more important, it is characteristic of the romantic image that it is "an aesthetic monad," original and rich in suggestion, but superior in its organic aliveness to any sort of limiting "discursive truth" about it.[6] To paraphrase, to translate, to explain the image is to debase and destroy the ineffable vision which cannot be communicated save through symbolic language.

It is probable that if Paul had tried to tell his parents and the doctor about the snow, they would have pronounced him mad, and Paul and his vision would thus have been sacrificed in vain. Therefore Paul willingly elects the sacrifice of himself alone by keeping his silence. He chooses the "timeless, shapeless, world-wide ideas." At once the reward of his ethical commitment is vouchsafed, a new and even more beautiful revelation. Ironically, just as the crisis /127/ seems to be over, this new revelation is interrupted by the harsh, mundane light; and it is Paul's mother, not his father, against whom he must cry out his rejection of even the well-meaning sensible world when it would seek to cut off his vision and deprive him of his truth. When the flower becomes seed in Paul's new revelation, Jones interprets the image as evidence of the "maturity process arrested, even diminishing. . . ." Jones is right, in one sense. Paul himself is the flower that becomes seed: he has flourished as an artist, and he must die rather than "mature" into perhaps another Mr. Hasleman. But the seed is a rich image that suggests also that Paul holds Infinity in the palm of his hand.

[6]Kermode, p. 44.

When eternity becomes accommodated to its containing artistic symbol, the artist achieves his ultimate cold peace. /128/

DISCUSSION QUESTIONS

1. What evidence do you find that suggests that Paul is indeed a symbol of the artist?

2. Landman suggests that Paul's artistic vision "becomes a screen that covers with beauty the ugliness of the world of particulars." To what extent does his vision cover ugliness with beauty? Is the snow itself beautiful? How is it described?

3. How convincing is Landman's explanation of the seed image at the end of the story?

THOMAS L. ERSKINE

The Two Worlds
of "Silent Snow,
Secret Snow"

Conrad Aiken, an early convert to the teachings of Freud, effectively portrays in "Silent Snow, Secret Snow" a young boy's psychological affliction. In criticism of the story one inevitably finds reference to "neurosis," "psychosis," "Oedipal complex," "schizophrenia," terms which critics use to describe the content, or subject, of the story. That the short story is more than a clinician's case study of a patient is obvious if one contrasts it to Hall's fictitious language-of-science version of the story.[1] As Clifton Fadiman points out, although the story could not have been written before the advent of psychiatry, Aiken treats his subject in an "unclinical" manner.[2] Arguing for an interpretation of Paul as artist, Ann Landman states that the psychological criticism of the story merely reflects the "laboratory knowledge" of the world, and then she offers a "symbolic" reading of the "facts" of the story.[3] While I have reservations about Mrs. Landman's reading of the story, I do share her belief that the symbolism in the story is literary as well as psychological. It is this "blend of the symbolic and the psychological," as Reuel Denny calls it,[4] which removes the story from the case history genre and qualifies it as an excellent short story.

An example of the symbolic and psychological simultaneously

[1]See Lawrence Hall, How Thinking Is Written (Boston, 1963), pp. 286–288.

[2]Reading I've Liked (New York, 1941), p. 734.

[3]" 'Silent Snow, Secret Snow': The Child as Artist," in Studies in Short Fiction, vol. I (1963), pp. 123–128.

[4]Conrad Aiken (Minneapolis, 1964), p. 14.

at work is Aiken's use of the "two different worlds" motif, which most critics mention only in passing. The motif is explicit: "But how then, between the two worlds, of which he was thus constantly aware, was he to keep a balance?" "Balance" is important psychologically because the term describes Paul's precarious hold on reality, but the nature of the two worlds and Paul's attitude toward them are conveyed symbolically in the story by the geography and explorer imagery. Like Keats' "On First Looking into Chapman's Homer," the short story concerns discovery.

In the first paragraph of his story Aiken juxtaposes the two worlds, portrays them, and suggests the image of Paul as explorer. For Paul, the snow world is a "delicious" secret, which he savors because it gives him a sense of both possession and protection: "It was as if, in some delightful way, his secret gave him a fortress, a wall behind which he could retreat into heavenly seclusion." The reference to "fortress," "wall," and "retreat" suggest the need to flee from the real world and also anticipate the hostility Paul sees during the "inquisition" (he refers to his parents and the doctor as "hostile presences"). The snow world is compared to a series of objects, which possess individuality, uniqueness, and almost, because of their protective function, a magical quality. On the other hand, the real world of the school is stylistically depicted as humdrum and dull by Aiken's prose: "The green and yellow continents passed and repassed, questions were asked and answered...."

In the first paragraph Paul moves from his snow world to the real world, but he does so through the use of Deirdre as reference point. Like a navigator at sea, Paul charts his course by the stars: "Deirdre, who had a funny little constellation of freckles on the back of her neck, exactly like the Big Dipper...." At the end of Part I Paul is again returned to reality through the bell and Deirdre: "He saw Deirdre rise, and had himself risen almost as soon—but not quite as soon—as she."

The geography lesson, which occupies the bulk of Part I, serves to sharpen the contrast between the two worlds and to develop Paul's role as explorer. The boundary lines between the two worlds are established by Miss Buell, who stresses the "imaginary" quality of the line about the middle of the earth. During the remainder of the lesson Miss Buell deals with geographical facts; Paul deals with his ideas about those facts. Paul's attention focuses on the white regions, the Arctic and Antarctic; but Miss Buell begins in the tropics, which are in green and which reflect life, even fertility (the animals and birds are like *"living"* jewels). As Paul thinks about the postman, the harbinger of the snow world, and of the peace, remoteness, cold, and sleep the snow world offers, Miss Buell moves north from the tropics to the "vast wheat-growing areas in North America and Siberia." When she reaches the Arctic region, she describes it as the "land of perpetual snow," a land which lacks fertility and life. How inadequately her brief one-liner describes Paul's land of enchantment!

In the course of Part I Paul finds it increasingly difficult to maintain the balance between his two worlds. In fact, he ironically must use "illusion" to remain in the real world:

> Each day it was more difficult to go through the perfunctory motions of greeting Mother and Father at breakfast, to reply to their questions, to put his books together and go to school. And at school, how extraordinarily hard to conduct with success simultaneously the public life and the life that was secret.

As Paul puts it, "It was as if he were trying to lead a double life." He prefers the snow world:

> He had to explore this new world which had been opened to him. Nor could there be the slightest doubt —not the slightest—that the new world was the profounder and more wonderful of the two. It was irresistible. It was miraculous. Its beauty was simply beyond anything—beyond speech as beyond thought—utterly incommunicable.

The decision to "explore" the new world significantly occurs just after Miss Buell tells the class about Hendrick Hudson's search for the Northwest Passage and after a discussion with his mother about geography (history, the recording of the past, is "dull"), the North Pole, and explorers like Peary, Scott, and Shackleton. The allusions are instructive: Scott reached the South Pole, but he perished on the return trip; Hudson searched for a passage to the Orient, a region seen as exotic and beautiful, but, as

Paul answers, Hudson was "disappointed." By mentioning Scott and Hudson, Aiken suggests that explorations like Paul's sometimes involve failure and death.

In Part II Aiken again implicitly compares Paul with an explorer, this time Columbus, who likewise sought a new route to the Orient, but found something else. On an odyssey of his own, Paul walks homeward (and Aiken's question "Homeward?" suggests Paul's "home" may not be with his parents) and sees a gateway, which itself is symbolic of passage from one world to another:

> Then came the gateway with two posts surmounted by egg-shaped stones which had been cunningly balanced on their ends as if by Columbus, and mortared in the very act of balance: a source of perpetual wonder. On the brick wall just beyond, the letter H had been stencilled, presumably for some purpose. H? H.

The details, presumably there for Aiken's purpose, suggest the identification of Paul Hasleman with Columbus, the precarious nature of the balance, the juxtaposition of two worlds, and the association of the egg-shaped stones with birth and, paradoxically, death.

The epiphany is particularly appropriate, because it is as a result of his journey homeward that he becomes increasingly interested in "miracles" rather than in the ugly details of daily life. In a richly evocative passage, the "items of mere externality" assume symbolic roles:

> Dirty sparrows huddled in the bushes, as dull in color as dead fruit left in leafless trees. A single starling creaked on a weather vane. In the gutter, beside a drain, was a scrap of torn and dirty newspaper, caught in a little delta of filth: the word ECZEMA appeared in large capitals, and below it was a letter from Mrs. Amelia D. Cravath, 2100 Pine Street, Fort Worth, Texas, to the effect that after being a sufferer for years she had been cured by Caley's Ointment. In the little delta, beside the fan-shaped and deeply runneled continent of brown mud, were lost twigs, descended from their parent trees, dead matches, a rusty horse-chestnut burr, a small concentration of sparkling gravel on the

lip of the sewer, a fragment of eggshell, a streak of yellow sawdust which had been wet and now was dry and
congealed, a brown pebble, and a broken feather.

The images suggest dirt and filth (the sparrows, newspaper, delta),
isolation ("a single starling" who "creaks," not sings), death ("dead
matches"), and sterility (the "rusty horse-chestnut burr," the
"fragment of eggshell" [particularly effective when contrasted with
the balanced "egg-shaped stones"]). Some of the items also seem
to demand a symbolic interpretation. Paul is like a "lost twig"
descended from parent trees, and in his crippled emotional state
("broken feather") he is on the brink of losing his balance (like
the "sparkling gravel on the lip of the sewer"). All the details,
including the ECZEMA advertisement with its adult hypocrisy
and false promise of "cures," serve as a microcosm of the real world
that Paul would leave. After all, the tiny patch of mud becomes a
"delta" and even a "continent," implying its universal application.

The real world accordingly turns Paul away, and while his snow
world becomes more extensive, the real world contracts. On the
walk home, for example, he sees the real world, but "something,"
the snow world, "teases" at the corner of his eyes and mind. The
process of shutting out the real world progresses rapidly in Part II,
and the "audible compass of the world" narrows until in Part III
the snow world eventually rules him.

From Paul's eyes the eye examination is an "inquisition," but
Aiken chooses to present extensive dialogue without editorial comment, without criticism. From a reading of the dialogue we view
the eye examination objectively: two concerned parents with a
doctor's help attempt, somewhat foolishly but not maliciously, to
find out what is "wrong" with their son. Yet Paul, who now sees
everything with snow-affected eyes, terms the examination a "cross-
examination," as well as an "inquisition." From his point of view,
the real world is phony, prosaic ("gross intelligences," "humdrum
minds"), but also threatening (his father's "punishment" voice).
In his paranoid condition the real is false, the illusion real. He even
believes that there is "proof" of his world, while the material
"proof" seen by the impartial observer testifies against Paul.

Except for his mother's brief appearance, Paul spends most of
Part IV in the snow world. The "audible compass of the world"

shuts out everything: we don't hear any noises from the real world. On the other hand, the hiss of the snow breaks into a roar. So complete is his citizenship in the snow world that he regards his mother's entrance as "something alien," something "hostile" from another world, which he can hardly understand. It is significant that he does remember the "exorcising words" which sever the cord between mother and son.

In these last moments, however, Aiken's imagery reflects his earlier use of the explorer motif. Paul as navigator is in his room, where "the bare black floor was like a little raft tossed in waves of snow." The "enormous whispering sea-waves" seem to swallow up the raft. In this final scene Aiken evokes an image of a young boy who seeks to discover a new world, although he is out of his depth, without a guide, with only a fragile, precarious craft. He finds peace, remoteness, cold, sleep, but he may also have found, by our reckoning, insanity or death.

GEORGE CICALA
JOHN McLAUGHLIN

A *Clinical Evaluation*
of a
Literary Character

Dallas Mental Hygiene Clinic
Dallas, Texas

Confidential Psychological Report
Patient: Paul Hasleman
Age: 12
Parents: Mr. & Mrs. Norman Hasleman
Admission Date: December 14, 1931
Referring Physician: S. Howells, M.D.

Paul entered the examination room accompanied by an attendant who found it necessary to guide Paul manually into the examinee's chair. Attempts to establish rapport were not totally unsatisfactory. The patient answered simple questions with replies which were vague and distracted, but upon prolonged and repeated questioning, gave appropriate answers. Attempts to administer conventional intelligence tests and personality inventories were abandoned when it became apparent that the inattentiveness of the patient precluded standardized test administration.

The psychiatric interview, on the other hand, was quite revealing. The distracted nature of the patient's comments and the constriction of verbal behavior suggested that the preferred diagnosis, based solely on the interview, should be incipient schizophrenia of the simple adient type, adience being suggested by the attractiveness of Paul's fantasy life. When Paul was questioned about his

George Cicala and John McLaughlin are Associate Professors of Psychology at the University of Delaware.

failure to answer immediately routine personal questions, he seemed impatient with the examiner and at one point in the interview blurted, "The snow ... I need the snow." In pursuing this comment, the sense of the patient's statements had to be gleaned from disjointed and confusing remarks, literally forced from him. It quickly became apparent that Paul possesses an imaginary world of a nurturing and enveloping snow-like medium, peopled with comforting voices. It seems likely that this fantasy world has become increasingly favored over that of the harsh realities of budding adolescence. This picture is totally consistent with adient schizophrenic detachment, and this diagnosis receives further support from Dr. Howells' description of increasing inattention to reality. It is our interpretation that Paul's failure to attend to reality is a function of his attentiveness to the internal cues of his fantasy and is therefore autistic.

A dynamic interpretation of the patient's fantasy would suggest that unresolved sexual conflict might have contributed to the onset of the detachment. The womb-like characteristics of the fantasy suggest a regressive escape, insulating Paul from the conflicts of adolescent sexuality. Play therapy was used to investigate the dynamics of this case. He played distractedly without apparent involvement, and we were impressed with his failure to follow through with activities symbolic of sexuality. He began at one point to construct a tunnel in sand only to abandon it with the excuse that he had lost interest. Similarly, his clay constructions would take on an initial concavity, only to be quickly modified. From behaviors such as these it was inferred that Paul's normal interest in sexual objects is being replaced by his more comfortable and comforting fantasy. At another point another impressive indicator of sexual conflict occurred. Paul rolled out the clay to an elongated phallic shape and then set it aside as though his play were completed. Later, when putting the clay away, Paul ignored the elongated piece of clay. When asked about it, he replied that it was not his. This incident suggests Paul's unwillingness to identify himself with masculine objects.

A number of times during the interview, Paul's future as an adult was discussed. On each occasion, Paul lapsed into his fantasy. Apparently denying his inevitable adult sexuality.

Unfortunately, prognosis in such cases is not favorable. It is likely that Paul will completely withdraw into his fantasy. This is further supported by the parents' refusal to permit immediate hospitalization and extensive therapy.

George A. Cicala
George A. Cicala, Ph.D.

John P. McLaughlin
John P. McLaughlin, Ph.D.

DISCUSSION QUESTION

In her opening paragraph Landman mentions the diagnosis that the doctor who examined Paul might have given. Does the diagnosis offered by Cicala and McLaughlin rest on the "facts" a doctor would have access to? What details of the story have Cicala and McLaughlin chosen to emphasize?

LAWRENCE HALL

Case History
of P. H.

     P.H. was a boy patient aged 14, an only child. Investigation showed he had always been somewhat aloof and withdrawn. He seldom entered into group activities. This does not appear to have been the result of shyness. In playing some ball games he showed as much ability as any child of comparable age to give and take. Adults who knew him seemed to feel that he had poise, but that somehow he lacked interest in all but a few pursuits.

     For example, he had a collector's instinct. He was always carrying trinkets of some sort—bits of shiny metal, odd shaped stones, or shells. This would not have struck anyone as peculiar except that he never manifested any desire to show the collected items to other people. On the contrary, he was very secretive about them. He would carry them around in his pocket, or in a bag or box, and drawing apart from human activity around him contemplate them for extended periods. If anyone showed interest in the items, he hastily stowed them away, and when asked questions about them he gave evasive answers as if reluctant to discuss them with anyone.

     His parents noticed several things which they thought unusual in a child his age. He was oblivious to much that went on around him. His mother called this daydreaming and absentmindedness. Occasionally she found it so hard to get his attention that she was afraid he might /286/ be getting deaf, and had his hearing tested by a physician. Unlike other children of her acquaintance he appeared glad to go to bed and even to take naps during the day, though he did not as a rule seem especially fatigued or sleepy. It

Reprinted by permission of the publisher, from Lawrence Hall, *How Thinking Is Written* (Lexington, Mass.: D. C. Heath and Company, 1963).

bothered her, she said, because he never got out of bed in the morning of his own accord, but seemed quite content to lie there awake indefinitely. It was obviously an effort for him to get dressed, washed, and participate in family affairs.

At school his work was generally good, although his teachers complained of inattention. They found it hard to account for his excellent recitations after having to call him three or four times before he realized he was to recite. He gave evidence simultaneously of being far away yet of being very accurately aware of what was going on. The principal felt that his grades, though good, "could have been even better."

Finally his seclusiveness and remoteness became so alarmingly strange that his parents called in the psychiatrist. The interview is described by him as follows:

> Physical examination was non-contributory. Hearing normal. Patient submitted without irregularity to interview. He showed mannerisms—averted glance, frequent grimaces, inappropriate smiling, and foolish laughing. He was correctly oriented and answered all questions deliberately and in a flat tone of voice. His conversation was relevant and coherent, but very careful as if he were concealing something. He denied hallucinations, delusions, or anxiety. When pressed he admitted to being preoccupied. He said: "I'm all right. I'm only thinking. You know what that is." Asked what he was thinking about, he replied, "Nothing special. Just something I know about. You wouldn't understand it. That's the thing of it. Nobody would. Epecially Mother and Dad. That's why I like to think about it. Because it's only thought by me." Finally he requested to be left alone and complained that he had just got a headache. "I don't like questions. They always make my head ache."

The psychiatrist diagnosed the condition as a schizophrenic reaction and recommended hospitalization. The next evening the patient's mother entered his bedroom and inquired if he was all right or if he wanted anything. Then he began to scream at her and suddenly "went into a trance."

Two days later P.H. was committed to a private hospital in an almost mute condition. On the third day after admission electro-shock treatments were instituted. /287/

Subsequent interviews indicated possible cause for emotional disturbance. While the view of informants had been that the family circle was an unusually comfortable and happy one, it appears that the parents, both of whom were musicians, were so uncommonly wrapped up in each other and their mutual interests that the patient, though much affection was lavished on him, sensed a great and mysteriously intimate communion between his mother and father which he craved to share but naturally could not. /288/

DISCUSSION QUESTIONS

1. What evidence is there for the statement that both parents were musicians and that Paul felt he could not share in the "great and mysterious intimate communion" that his parents possessed?

2. What does the "language of science" lack that the "language of literature" possesses?

THE FILM

Introduction to
the Shot Analysis

The *shot analysis* is an interpretive transcript of a film based on its final edited version as seen by the theater audience. It is superior to the *shooting script* of the film in that it describes the finished work rather than the filmmaker's projected plans for the finished work. Naturally, no verbal description can actually duplicate the experience of seeing the film, but the shot analysis allows one to carefully analyze the film after having seen it.* Film critics sometimes err in their factual description of a particular film, and such errors often destroy their carefully reasoned analyses. The shot analysis also allows one to reconsider certain visual constructs and key speeches when repeated screenings of the film would not be practical. Finally, many films are so carefully formed and so densely textured that the shot analysis enables the viewer to investigate directorial subtleties that may not be apparent, even after a number of screenings of the film. For all of these reasons, the shot analysis must verbally record the sound, the visuals, and the structuring of the film in a meaningful way, and this is made possible through a kind of descriptive shorthand.

*Silent Snow, Secret Snow" is available for inexpensive rental or sale from CCM Films Inc., 34 MacQuesten Parkway South, Mount Vernon, New York, 10550; Film Center Inc., 20 East Huron St., Chicago, Ill., 60611; and Western Cinema Guild, Inc., 244 Kearny St., San Francisco, Calif. 94108.

SHOT

A *shot* is a reproduction of an image from the time the camera starts to the time it stops. It may be shortened by eliminating the beginning and/or end of the resulting strip of film. In the shot analysis, each shot is numbered and the designated number precedes the description. When a given shot is a duplication of one found earlier, this is noted [e.g., 34 (=18)]. At the end of each shot description, duration is given in seconds or rough fractions of seconds [e.g., (1].

KINDS of SHOTS

Shots are conventionally described as *long* (LS), *medium* (MS), or *close-up* (CU). The long shot would show the bodies of one or more people, the medium shot would show one or more people, usually from the waist up, the close-up would show the head and shoulders of one person. On occasion, these shots are described as being *medium* (M) or *extreme* (E). Thus, if a shot presents us with a panoramic view of nature or a view of a person's eyes, the following descriptions would be appropriate: ELS, ECU. Another shot could show a person from the chest up: MCU.

SHOT TRANSITIONS

Shots are joined or edited together in various ways, usually by cuts. Here, one image is immediately replaced by another. Since the *cut* is the usual method of shot change, it is not noted in the analysis. Fades and dissolves are noted as they occur. A *fade-in* transition begins with a black screen, gradually becoming light until the next shot is seen. A *fade-out* transition gradually darkens the scene until the screen is black. When a transition is termed a *dissolve*, one shot is seen to fade-out while the next shot fades-in. At the midpoint of such a transition, the two shots can be seen as superimpositions. While the duration of the cut transition is always uniform, the duration of fades and dissolves is not.

CAMERA MOVEMENT

The camera may be moved within a shot in various ways. It may *pan* (move horizontally on a fixed axis), *tilt* (move vertically on a fixed axis), or do both at the same time. In the analysis this latter movement is called a *diagonal*. The cameraman may carry out these movements at any speed he desires. Very fast movement is termed a *zip*. Other camera movements may be achieved by bodily moving the camera as well as its axis. This is called a *track*, since it was usually carried out in the early days of the film by actually placing the camera on tracks. At present, however, tracking is most often done by placing the camera and its axis on a rubber-tired vehicle. Some use the term *travel* to indicate that the tracking shot is moving at a different speed than the object being photographed. A tracking shot of a fixed object is sometimes called a *dolly*. No distinction has been made between tracking, traveling, and dollying in this analysis. Finally, the *zoom-lens* is sometimes used to produce movement similar to a track.

CAMERA ANGLES

The camera can be set up prior to the shot or moved during the shot to obtain certain angles. The shot in which the camera is parallel to the subject is considered the norm and is not noted in the analysis. In a *low-angle shot*, the camera is tilted upward on its axis; in a *high-angle shot*, the camera is tilted downward.

SOUND

Since the shots in this film are relatively short, no attempt has been made to intersperse the visual description with the dialogue or to specify the exact points within the duration of the shot where musical or naturalistic sounds begin and end.

As was noted at the beginning of this introduction, the shot analysis should not be thought of as a duplication of the experience of seeing the film. Many of the descriptions of the visuals and sounds are subjective and selective. Thus, it is conceivable that another shot analysis of this film would emphasize certain visual elements or interpret certain speeches in different ways. Hopefully, however, distortions have been kept at a minimum.

Shot 5. All stills used with the permission of Brandon Films.

GERALD R. BARRETT and
THOMAS L. ERSKINE

Shot Analysis:
"Silent Snow,
Secret Snow"

1 Fade in. LS. On right a tree with almost bare branches
forming a web-like design. Credits are superimposed on
the shot. Music (cello, flute, and harp). (These instru-
ments are played at various times throughout the film,
usually solo.)

> SILENT SNOW,
> SECRET SNOW
>
> by
> CONRAD AIKEN
>
> Produced by
> GENE KEARNEY
> ALEXANDER ALLAND
> RICHARD TOMPKINS

Dissolve (15

2 LS. On left a similar tree. Credits are superimposed on
the shot. Music.

> Featuring
> SIMON GIRARD
>
> with
> FRANK NIXON, CHASE CROSBY
> MARY MUENZEN, WILLIAM MILES

Dissolve (6

3   LS. A closer view of the tangled branches. Credits are superimposed on the shot. Music.

> Music Composed
> and Conducted by
> GEORGE KLEINSINGER
>
> Narration by MICHAEL KEENE
> Photographed and Edited by
> GENE KEARNEY
>
> Technical Assistance:
> FRED BURRELL, RICHARD VAN ZANDT,
> MARY MILES, JAMES SIGNORELLI

Dissolve   (11½

4   (=1) Credits are superimposed on the shot. Music.

> Adapted for the screen
> and Directed by
> GENE KEARNEY

Dissolve   (8

5   LS from low angle of the tops of several trees. Pan right and tilt up focusing on one tree. Pan right so that a network of branches appears. Music.

> Narrator: Just why it should have happened, or why it should have happened just when it did, he could not, of course, possibly have said; nor perhaps would it even have occurred to him to ask. The thing was above all a secret, something to be preciously concealed; and to that very fact it owed an enormous part of its deliciousness.

Dissolve   (21

6   CU of globe and two hands which turn the globe. Both hands withdraw from globe.

Teacher (off camera): Deirdre, perhaps you can tell us what the equator is.   (5½

7   CU of Deirdre in the classroom.
Deirdre: The equator is a line that goes around the middle of the earth.

Teacher (off camera): Oh, I see. The earth is wearing a belt   (8

8   MS of students in the classroom. The smiling students look toward Deirdre.

Teacher (off camera): or a sash. Or someone   (2

9   (=7)
Teacher (off camera): drew a line around it.

Deirdre: No! No! Not that. I mean, well . . .

Teacher (off camera): Did you forget the word "imaginary"?

Deirdre: Yes.   (7

10 MS of Deirdre, who is standing. As she sits down in her seat, tilt down. Paul is half-hidden behind her. Track past Deirdre to a MCU of Paul. Paul's face is blank, expressionless, as if he were concentrating on something else. Music.

Narrator: It was as if in some delightful way the secret gave him a fortress, a wall behind which he could retreat in heavenly seclusion.   (10½

11 LS of the geography teacher standing at the blackboard, facing left, and pointing toward a large map of North America. Students are seated in the foreground. She points to the polar regions, turns to the class, and speaks. Music.

Teacher: Moving up to the Arctic Circle we again enter a zone of perpetual snow.   (8

12 CU of Paul, who is staring down at his desk. He slowly raises his head and looks straight ahead. Music.

Narrator: All he needed to do was to think of that morning, the first one   (4

13   ECU of a globe. Camera focuses on polar regions and slowly zooms in. Music.

>   Narrator: and then of all the others.

>   Dissolve   (6½

14   LS of Paul's bedroom. Paul is lying in his bed. As camera pans a bit to the right, he turns and we see his face. Music.

>   Narrator: Suddenly for no reason he had thought of the postman. He remembered the postman. Perhaps there was nothing so odd in that.   (5½

15   LS from high angle (Paul's bedroom window) of Paul's street seen through a network of branches. At the end of the street a postman is entering the first house. Music.

>   Narrator: After all, he heard the postman almost every morning of his life. His heavy boots could be heard   (7

16   MS from foot of Paul's bed of Paul, who is lying in his bed. Music.

>   Narrator: clomping around the corner at the bottom of the little hill street,   (3½

17   (=15) The postman crosses the street and walks diagonally across the street and off camera right. Music. Sound of postman's steps.

>   Narrator: and then progressively nearer, progressively louder,   (5

18   CU of Paul, who is still lying in bed and whose face is illuminated against a dark background. Music.

>   Narrator: the double knock at each door, the crossings   (3½

19   (=15) Camera follows postman as he recrosses the street. Music.

>   Narrator: and recrossings of the street   (2½

Shot 17.

20   (=18) Paul opens his eyes and turns his head to the
     window behind him. Music.

       Narrator: until finally the clumsy steps came   (2½

21   LS from high angle (Paul's window) of the postman
     seen through branches of a tree as he recrosses the street
     towards Paul's house. Music.

       Narrator: stumbling across to the very door   (2½

22   CU of postman's feet. Camera pans left as he walks on
     sidewalk. Camera stops and after he walks off camera left,
     camera remains focused on the sidewalk and on the adja-
     cent fallen leaves and grass. Music.

       Narrator: and the tremendous knock that shook the
       house itself.

     KNOCK!   (4

23   (=12) CU of Paul at his desk.

     KNOCK!   (2

24   MS from low angle of the teacher, who is facing the
     class, standing in front of the blackboard, and reading
     from a book. Deirdre, who is in the foreground right,
     scratches the back of her neck.

     Teacher: These constitute the vast wheat-growing areas
     in North America   (4½

25   (=12) CU of Paul at his desk.

     Teacher (off camera): and Siberia.   (2

26   MCU of Deirdre, who scratches the back of her neck and
     then stops. Music.

       Narrator: But on that particular morning, the first
       morning,   (4

27   (=16) MS of Paul, who is lying in his bed. Music.

       Narrator: he had for some reason waited for the
       postman;   (3½

28 (=14) LS of Paul's bedroom. Paul is lying in his bed. He rolls over on his back and stretches out his arms. Music.

>   Narrator: but when at last the steps were heard they had already come round the corner a little up the hill to the first house;   (6

29 (=18) CU. Paul opens his eyes and looks toward window. Music.

>   Narrator: and even so they were curiously different and he had understood the situation at once. Nothing could have been simpler.   (8

30 LS of snow-covered street. Music.

>   Narrator: There had been snow in the night such as all season   (4

31 (=18) CU of Paul in bed as he looks toward window. Music.

>   Narrator: he had been hoping for,   (2

32 LS of postman, who walks along snow-covered street, opens gate, and enters yard of Paul's house. Music.

>   Narrator: and it was this which had rendered the postman's first steps inaudible and the later ones faint, and even now it   (6½

33 MS from low angle. Pan with postman to door of Paul's house. Music.

>   Narrator: must be snowing. The white ragged lines

KNOCK! KNOCK!   (2½

34 (=18) CU of Paul, who looks toward window. Music.

>   Narrator: drifting and sifting,   (2

35 LS of postman, who closes gate in front of boy's house and walks across street past panning camera. Camera stops after he walks off left, remaining focused on a hill covered with snow and weeds. Music. Sound of storm.

Narrator: whispering and hushing, seething and getting deeper and deeper, silenter and silenter.   (9

36   CU from high angle of footsteps in snow. Tilt up to snow-covered field and lower toward trees in distance. Tilt up trunks of trees. Music. Sound of storm.   (6½

37   MS of large bare bush in field of snow in foreground, right section of frame. Larger trees in background. Tilt up to interlaced branches. Music. Sound of storm.   (7

38   LS of branches in tops of trees. Tilt down to ground. Music. Sound of storm.   Dissolve   (5½

39   LS from low angle of trees with snow-covered concrete urn on wall in foreground. Tilt down and pan to trees. Music. Sound of storm.   (4½

40   MS of fir branches half-buried in snow. Music.   (3

41   (=18) CU. Paul gets out of bed and moves off camera. Camera remains focused on his white pillow and the impression made by his head (impression resembles branches).   (3½

42   MS of Paul wearing pajamas and staring out his bedroom window. Pan right with Paul, who moves to window and pulls curtain aside.   (5½

43   MS of Paul from outside his bedroom window. Sunlight glares on the window and reflections of branches can be seen.   (1½

44   LS from high angle of Paul's street as seen from his bedroom window. The street is bathed in sunlight; there is no snow. Pan right up the street (=15).   (5

45   CU of Paul at window. Sunlight and trees are reflected off the window.   (3

46   (=14) LS. Paul is looking out window, then moves back from window and sits on edge of his bed. He stares into space. Music.

Narrator: Queer, the effect this extraordinary surprise had upon him. All the following morning

Dissolve   (7½

47   LS. Pan with Paul putting on his coat and moving to
breakfast table. His father, dressed in business suit, holds
morning paper and cup and looks at Paul. Paul's mother
enters from kitchen and puts plates on table. She and
Paul sit down with father. Music.

Narrator: he had kept with him a sense as of snow
falling about him, a secret screen of new snow between himself and the world.   (6

48   MS of Paul, though his father's paper is visible on left in
corner of frame. Paul pulls his chair closer to the table,
sits back, and reaches for a glass of milk. He holds the
glass, stares at it, but doesn't drink it. Music.

Narrator: If he had not dreamed such a thing (and
how could he have dreamed it while awake?) how
else could one   (7

49   CU of Paul sliding glass of milk across table toward himself. His father's right hand and paper are in background.
Paul moves the glass toward himself and then puts his
left hand around the glass. Tilt up over glass and paper
to father's face. He looks up from his paper, smiles in-
dulgently at Paul, and returns to his paper. Music.

Narrator: explain it? He could not now remember
whether it was on the first or the second morning.
Or was it even the third that his mother had   (9½

50   MS of Paul in profile. He holds the glass of milk. After
looking in his father's direction, he returns to gazing at
the glass of milk and then looks at his mother. Music.

Narrator: drawn attention to some oddness in his
manner?   (4½

51   MS of Paul's mother serving breakfast.   (2½

Shot 42

Shot 45.

52 (=50) Paul holds glass of milk in both hands, then
raises it to his lips and drinks.

Mother (off camera): Paul.   (3½

53 (=51) Paul's mother looks at him, extends her left
hand, draws it back a bit, and then extends it again.

Mother (more loudly): Paul, dear, you   (4½

54 MCU of Paul's father, who looks in Paul's direction.   (1½

55 CU of Paul's mother.   (1½

56 MCU of Paul, who holds the glass of milk in his hand
and does not appear to be listening. He looks up at his
mother.

Mother (off camera): don't seem to be listening.

Father (off camera): What   (2

57 (=26) MCU. Deirdre scratches the back of her neck.

Father (off camera) in exasperated tones: the devil is it,
Paul?   (1½

58 (=12) CU. Paul in his classroom.

Mother (off camera): Paul!

Teacher (off camera): Now does anyone know   (2

59 Teacher (off camera): the difference between the North
Pole and the magnetic pole?

(=26) MCU from behind Deirdre. She raises her hand,
as do the other students, to answer the question. Tilt up
Deirdre's arm to MS of teacher.

Narrator: Perhaps it   (6

60 (=12) CU of Paul, who looks up from his desk.

Narrator: hadn't been on the second or   (1½

61 ECU of Deirdre's hand which she is waving in the air.
The waving hand suggests the fluttering of a bird.

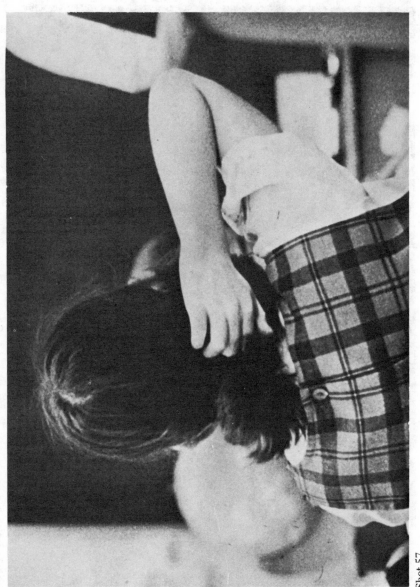

Shot 57.

Shot 63.

> Narrator: third morning or even the fourth or fifth.
> How could he be sure? How could he be sure just
> when the (6½

62 (=18) CU of Paul in bed. He turns his head and opens
his eyes.

> Narrator: delicious progress had become clear, just
> when it had really begun? All he knew was that at
> some point or another, perhaps the second day, per-
> haps the sixth, he had noticed that the presence of
> the snow was a little more insistent, the sound of it
> clearer and conversely the sound of the postman's
> steps more indistinct.

Music. (21

63 LS of postman walking up snow-covered street. Postman
is partly obscured by out-of-focus branches in foreground.
Postman walks off camera. Music. Sound of postman's
steps.

> Narrator: Not only could he not hear the steps
> come around the corner, he could not even hear
> them at the first house. It was above the first house
> that he heard them and then a few days later above
> the second and a few days later above (12½

64 CU pan of postman's feet as he walks up the street
(=22). Music. Sound of steps grows louder.

> Narrator: the third. Gradually, gradually, the snow
> was becoming heavier, the sound of the seething
> louder, the footsteps more and more muffled.

> Dissolve (13

65 CU of Paul peering out his window (similar to the end
of shot 42). Music.

> Narrator: When he found every morning on going
> to the window (3

66 (=44) LS from high angle of Paul's street bathed in sunlight. Music.

> Narrator: that the roads and the streets were   (2

67 (=43) MS of Paul from outside his bedroom window, sunlight and branches reflecting off window.
> Narrator: as bare as ever, it made no difference; this was, after all, what he had expected; it was even what pleased him, what rewarded him.

Music.   (9

68 MS. Paul's mother dressed in black. She stands in darkened doorway and lights a cigarette. Music.

> Narrator: There outside   (3

69 ECU of Paul's eyes. Music.

> Narrator: were the bare streets and here   (1½

70 LS from low angle of lighted cut-glass chandelier in a room on the first floor. Music.

> Narrator: inside was the snow,   (2½

71 CU of lighted cut-glass chandelier. Zoom in. Image gradually goes out of focus until last word of following is accompanied by a blur of light. Music.

> Narrator: snow growing heavier each day, muffling the world, hiding the ugly, and deadening increasingly, above all, the steps of the postman.

Mother (off camera): Paul,   (14½

72 (=68) Paul's mother turns in his direction.

Mother: your father thinks you might need a new lamp upstairs for your study.

Father (off camera): We've been   (6

73 ECU (out of focus) of bottom half of the chandelier, moving and glittering.

Father (off camera): worrying, Paul; we thought maybe it was eyestrain that's been bothering you.   (5

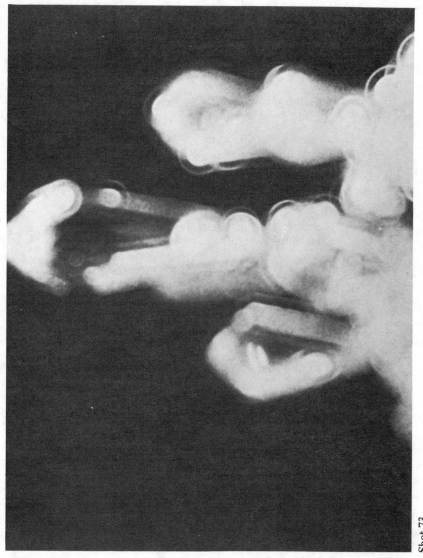

Shot 73.

74 (=69) ECU of Paul's eyes.

>   Narrator: How was one to explain? Would it be   (3

75 CU of Paul's father, who also looks in Paul's direction.

>   Narrator: safe to explain?   (2

76 CU of Paul in classroom.

>   Narrator: Would it merely mean that he would get into some obscure   (2½

77 MS of the teacher in profile. She points to the map: first to the southern part of the United States, then to the western mountain range, and then to northern Canada. During the shot we see her talking, but we do not hear her.

>   Narrator: kind of trouble? And how could he explain his new world?

>   Father (off camera): How's school going, son?   (6

78 MCU of Paul (from slight high angle), who is seated in a chair in the living room at his house. He faces his parents.

>   Father (off camera): History was my favorite subject.

>   Paul: I think I prefer geography, especially when it takes one to the North Pole.   (10

79 (=68) MS of Paul's mother.

>   Father (off camera): Why the North Pole?

>   Paul (off camera): Well,   (2½

80 (=78)

>   Paul: it would be fun to be an explorer, like Peary or Scott, or Byrd.   (6

81 (=68) MS of Paul's mother. Music.   (3

82 ECU of bottom half of chandelier, moving and glittering (similar to shot 73, but more blurred, out of focus). Music.

Narrator: It was irresistible, this new world: it was miraculous. Its beauty was (6½

83 (=12) CU. Paul's gaze shifts from left to right. Music.

Narrator: beyond anything, beyond speeches, beyond (3½

84 LS from low angle of storm clouds. Music.

Narrator: thought, like in the incommunicable, (2½

85 LS from high angle of snow-covered trees and shrubs. Tilt up to tops of trees. Music. Sound of storm.

Narrator: and with each passing day it increased. The snow became deeper, heavier; the sound of its seething more distinct, (9½

86 LS from low angle of snow-covered trees on the left. Music. Sound of storm.

Narrator: more soothing, (3

87 LS from low angle of a snow-covered tree on the right. Pan left until the camera focuses on several trees. Music. Sound of storm.

Narrator: more persistent. (5½

88 MCU of Deirdre (left), Paul (center), and another student (right), who is only partially visible (similar to shot 10). Track in to CU of Paul. Music. Sound of storm.

Teacher (off camera): Perhaps we'll ask Paul. (5

89 LS of the classroom. The teacher approaches Paul's desk and several students turn and look at him. (1

90 (=12) CU of Paul.

Teacher (off camera): Paul. (1

91 CU of teacher.

Teacher: Paul. (1½

92 MCU from low angle. Paul's mother bends down over Paul, who is lying in his bed.

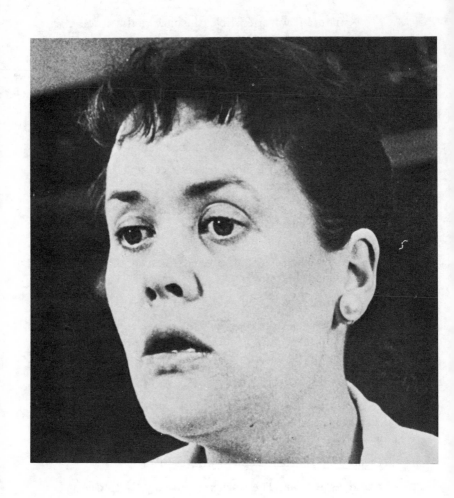

Shot 91.

Shot 92.

Mother: Paul, if this goes on we'll have to see a doctor. We can't have our boy living in another world so far away.

Paul turns abruptly away from her and stares into space.

> Narrator: There were times when he longed, positively ached, to burst out with it, to   (19½

93   MS from foot of Paul's bed. He lies in his bed. His gaze is averted from his mother, who pulls his blanket up to his shoulders and reaches over him to turn out the light in his room.

> Narrator: tell everyone about it, only to be checked almost at once by a sense of mysterious power in his very secrecy. It must   Fade out   (8½

94   (=12) CU. Paul stares vacantly and then looks up.

> Narrator: be kept secret.   (1½

95   LS from high angle (behind teacher) of Paul, who faces camera. The teacher walks towards Paul's desk.

> Narrator: That more and more became clear.   (2

96   CU of two of Paul's classmates: the boy rests his chin on his hands and looks down at his desk; the girl turns toward Paul and half-smiles.

> Narrator: At whatever cost to himself,   (2½

97   CU of Deirdre, who turns around to look in Paul's direction and smiles.

> Narrator: whatever pain   (1

98   (=12) CU. Paul stares into space, then looks down.

> Narrator: to others.

Teacher (off camera): Perhaps   (3

99   (=89) The teacher walks to Paul's desk and looks down at him. His classmates look at him and wait for his answer. Zoom in. Paul stands at his desk.

Teacher: you'll come out of your daydream long enough
to be able to tell us, won't you, Paul?

Paul: It is what we now call the   (6½

100 CU of Paul.

Paul: Hudson River.

Teacher: And?

Paul: He thought it was the Northwest Passage. He was
disappointed.

Teacher: Thank you.   (8½

101 LS. A schoolyard. A large tree in foreground in center of
frame and a group of children playing kickball. Pan right
to a girl kicking the ball. Laughter and shouts of children.
                                                             (6½

102 LS from high angle. The front of the school building as
seen through branches of a tree. Students leaving school
in small groups and talking with each other.   (6½

103 LS. Paul, against a dark, wooded background, walks by
himself along sidewalk. A rail fence is in foreground. Pan
right with Paul. Two boys enter frame, run shouting past
Paul, and go off camera. A boy on a bicycle also passes
him. Music.   (14

104 CU of Paul's legs as he walks on cracked sidewalk toward
tracking camera. Music.

      Narrator: On the walk homeward, which was time-
      less, it   (4½

105 LS tracking toward metal griffin, which is split in two
and is mounted on bases on either side of the stone steps.
Pan right to front view of griffin as tracking continues.
Music.

      Narrator: pleased him to see through the accom-
      paniment, or counterpoint, of snow the items of
      mere externality   (6

Shot 105.

106   LS from low angle of tree trunks and tree tops. Track
      past trees and tilt up to 90°. Music.

               Narrator: on his way.   (6½

107   (=104) Music.   (5½

108   MS. Paul walks right. Camera tracks with Paul. Woods
      in background. Music.   (8½

109   MS of Paul, who has just crossed road. Road, cars, and
      woods in background. Pan left and more cars are visible.
      Tilt down as Paul bends over and sees a dead mouse lying
      in the gutter. Music.

               Narrator: Further   (3½

110   CU from high angle of dead mouse in dirt and water at
      curb. Paul's shadow in lower left of frame. Music.

               Narrator: on, further on,   (2

111   CU of Paul, who has his back to the camera. He turns
      and looks right. Music.

               Narrator: there was something else now further on   (3

112   LS of house and tree (right). Paul enters frame and runs
      up the street. Pan right with Paul. A second house. Paul
      runs off camera. Music.

               Narrator: which was already assuming the sharper
               importance. He knew what he was going to look at
               next. It was his own house, his own little hill-street,
               his silent, his secret snow.   (12½

113   LS of Paul running up the street. He is seen through a
      slatted fence in foreground. Pan right to end of fence and
      beyond to LS of Paul's street. Paul runs to middle of the
      intersection, stops, turns to his left, and looks up his
      street. Music.   (7

114   MCU from low angle of Paul. The sun glares over his
      shoulder. Vertical track upward, shutting out sunlight
      and showing Paul against a background of snow. Music.
                                                              (3½

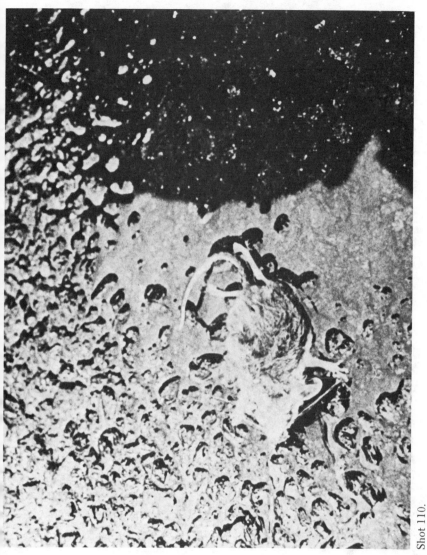

Shot 110.

Shot 113.

115   LS of Paul, who stands with his back to the camera. He looks up his street (the shot resembles the end of shot 113), but his street is now covered with snow. Music.   (2

116   CU from low angle of Paul, who looks up the street. A branch is overhead. Music. Sound of storm.   (3½

117   (=115) Paul runs up the snow-covered street. Music. Sound of storm.   (4

118   MS of Paul running up the street. Pan with Paul. Music. Sound of storm.   (3

119   (=117) Paul continues running up the street. Music. Sound of storm.   (4½

120   (=118) Paul runs, stumbles. Music. Sound of storm.   (2½

121   CU of snow-covered hedge. Pan left to LS of street from the top. Paul runs toward camera. Music. Sound of storm.   (5

122   MS of Paul running toward camera. Music. Sound of storm.   (1½

123   MS of picket fence across the street from Paul's house. Paul's shadow appears on fence, and then he runs on frame and looks back down the street. Music.   (4

124   MS of Paul turning and looking further up the street. He shakes his head and looks across the street and up to his room. Music.   (5

125   (=43) MS of Paul in pajamas. He looks out his window. Music.   (3

126   (=124) Zoom in to CU of Paul's face. Music.

      Narrator: This   (2½

127   MS of Paul's window (like shots 43 and 124, but this time Paul is not at the window). Music.

      Narrator: morning (could he be mistaken?)   (2½

Shot 115.

128   MS of Paul looking back down the street. Music.

       Narrator: it was just above the seventh   (1½

129   MCU of Paul, who quickly turns his back to the camera
and looks at his house. Abrupt diagonal to upper story
of house. Music.

       Narrator: house, his own house,   (2½

130   (=16) MS of Paul lying in his bed near the window.
Music.

       Narrator: that the postman had first been audible.
The knock he heard must have been the knocking
on his own door. The   (7½

131   (=129) Paul, who is looking at his room, moves ahead
toward camera. Music.

       Narrator: realization gave him abruptly and even a
little   (2½

132   LS of Paul standing in front of his house on the snow-
covered street. He runs across the street and enters his
house. Music.

       Narrator: frighteningly a sense of hurry. He was
being hurried, he was being rushed. Did it mean
(and this was an idea   (7½

133   CU of Paul in profile at door. He looks up at his house.
Music.

       Narrator: which gave him an extraordinary sense of
surprise) that he would never hear the postman
again? Was it all going to happen at the end, so suddenly, or indeed   (11

134   LS from low angle of the side of Paul's house, which is
not covered with snow. Music.

       Narrator: had it already happened?   (4½

135   ECU of Paul's mouth.

Paul: Ahhh.

Tilt up to an ECU of his eyes and nose.   (3

136 MS of Paul's father (foreground) dressed in a business suit. He is seated in an armchair in the living room and is reading the paper. Paul's mother is sewing in the background. Paul's father flicks an ash from his cigarette, and Paul's mother looks up from her sewing.

  Narrator: After supper the   (2

137 MS of Paul and doctor, who face each other. The doctor looks in Paul's mouth.

  Narrator: inquisition   (1

138 MCU of the doctor, who is examining Paul. The back of Paul's head is in foreground. The doctor's face is illuminated. The rest of the room, except for a lighted, globed lamp, is darkened. Paul's father's face is in left foreground. Paul's mother appears in dark background and moves to his father; she stands beside him and puts her hand on his chair. They look at the doctor and Paul.

  Narrator: began.

Doctor: And now take it slowly and, and, hold it if you can.

Paul: Ah-h-h-h—   (7½

139 ECU of Paul's eyes (similar to shot 135).

  Narrator: How silly all this   (2

140 MS of Paul's mother, who stands beside chair of the seated father. She moves into foreground toward the doctor, and her husband hands her a book.

  Narrator: was. As if it had anything to do with his throat or his heart or his lungs.   (5½

141 (=139)   (1½

142 ECU of Paul's mother, whose nose and eyes are illumnated against a dark background. She quickly turns her head toward the doctor.

Doctor (off camera): Now, Paul,   (3

143   CU from slightly low angle of the doctor; Paul facing
        doctor in foreground, mother looking on from the side.

        Doctor: I just want you to read this as you, as you,
        naturally would.   (3½

144   CU from slightly high angle of Paul reading from the
        book.

        Paul: And another praise have I to tell for this,   (4

145   (=143) Paul's father rises from his chair and becomes a
        threatening presence in the background.

        Paul: the city, our mother, the gift of the great god,   (3½

146   (=144)

        Paul: a glory of the land most high, the might of horses,
        the might of the sea. . . .   (5½

147   (=end of shot 145) The doctor turns to Paul's mother.

        Doctor: No, there is no sign of superficial eyestrain at
        all. We could have his eyes examined, but I believe it's
        something else.   (10

148   CU of Paul. Music.

        Narrator: Even here, even   (3

149   MCU of Paul's father against a dark background. He
        takes a drag from his cigarette. Part of the lighted lamp
        is in background. Music.

        Narrator: among these hostile presences,   (2

150   (=148) Paul turns his eyes away from the adults. Music.

        Narrator: the snow was awaiting, out of   (2½

151   MS of fireplace, where a fire is burning brightly. Brass
        andirons and fireplace utensils. Music.

        Narrator: sight, with a voice that said, "Wait,   (3½

152   (=139) ECU of Paul's eyes looking at the fire. Music.

        Narrator: Paul, just wait."   (1½

153 MS of Paul's father's chair, which is illuminated by a lamp off camera.

Doctor (off camera): Is there anything that worries you very much? (4½

154 (=148) CU of Paul. Paul nervously touches his right hand to his cheek.

Paul: Oh, no, I think not.

Doctor: Are you quite sure? You needn't answer at (6½

155 CU from low angle of Paul's father, who looks concerned, but also exasperated and angry.

Doctor (off camera): once, Paul. Remember we're trying to help you. (4

156 (=148) CU of Paul.

Doctor (off camera): Think it over (1½

157 (=155)

Doctor (off camera): and be quite sure, won't you?

Music.

Narrator (as sound of snow): "Wait, Paul, (4

158 (=148) CU of Paul. Music.

Narrator: just wait till we're alone together, and I will tell you something new, something (5½

159 (=70) LS from low angle of a cut-glass chandelier in a room on the first floor. Music.

Narrator: cold, something sleepy, something of (3

160 (=148) CU of Paul turning his head toward the ceiling. Music.

Narrator: cease, and peace (1

161 LS from low angle of corner of room where two walls meet ceiling. Music.

Narrator: and the long bright curve (2

162   (=135) ECU of Paul's eyes. He looks at the corner of
      the ceiling. Music.

         Narrator: of space. Banish   (2

163   MCU from low angle of Paul's mother (left), his father
      (center), and the doctor (right). The faces of the doctor
      and Paul's mother are illuminated; Paul's father's face is
      in semidarkness. All three look stern and forbidding.
      Music.

         Narrator: them. Refuse to speak. Leave them. Go   (4

164   MS from high angle of Paul looking up at the ceiling.
      The adults all look at Paul. Music.

         Narrator: upstairs to your room.   (1

165   (=148) CU from low angle of Paul looking up at ceil-
      ing. Music.

         Narrator: I will   (2

166   (=135) ECU of Paul's eyes. Music.

         Narrator: be waiting for you.   (1½

167   (=73) ECU (out of focus) of bottom half of chande-
      lier, moving and glittering. Music.

         Narrator: I will tell you a story better

                                        Dissolve   (3

168   LS of snow-covered field and woods. Music. Sound of
      storm.

         Narrator: than *The Snow Ghost*. I will surround
         your bed, close the windows, pile a deep drift against
         the door, so that none will ever enter. Speak to   (12

169   (=148) CU of Paul.

         Narrator: them."

      Paul: I'm just thinking.   (3½

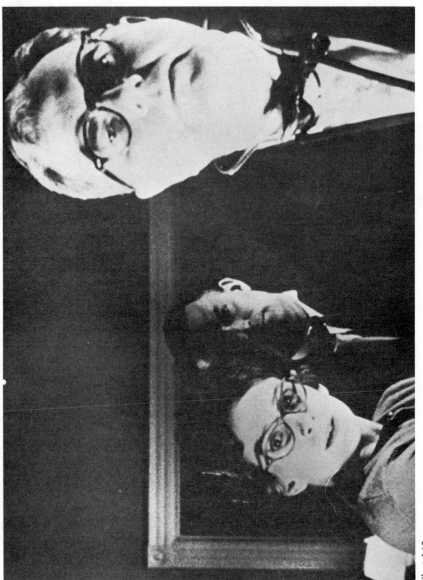

Shot 163.

170   (=163)

Mother: But, my dear, about what?   (2½

171   (=148) CU of Paul.

Paul: About what?

Mother (off camera): Yes, Paul,   (1½

172   (=155) CU of Paul's father.

Mother (off camera): about what?   (1

173   (=148) CU of Paul.

Paul: Anything.   (1½

174   CU of Paul's mother, who is visibly upset. She faces cam-
      era, turns abruptly to right when Paul laughs, and raises
      her left hand to her face in shock.

Father (off camera): Paul, you're making   (2

175   (=155) CU of Paul's father.

Father: this very painful for your mother. What are you
thinking about?   (4½

176   (=148) CU of Paul.   (3

177   CU of Paul's mother in foreground and his father in
      background. Again his father, unlike his mother, is in
      semidarkness.   (2

178   (=148) CU of Paul.

Paul: About the snow.   (2

179   (=177) Paul's mother turns to her husband and then
      back to Paul.

Father: What on earth!

Mother: But, my dear, what do you mean?   (5½

180 (=148) CU of Paul.

Paul: Just snow, that's all. I like to think about it.

Doctor (off camera): Tell us about   (5½

181 CU from low angle of the doctor, who seems threatening, ominous.

Doctor: it, my boy.

Paul (off camera): That's   (1½

182 (=148) CU of Paul.

Paul: all there is; there's nothing to tell. You know what snow is.   (4

183 (=163) MCU of Paul's parents and the doctor.   (1½

184 (=135) ECU of Paul's eyes. He looks up at ceiling.

      Narrator (as sound of snow): "Hurry, Paul, hurry, these last few precious hours."   (3½

185 (=164) MS of Paul, his parents, and the doctor.   (1½

186 (=148) CU of Paul.

Paul: Mother, can I go to bed now? Please.   (2

187 (=177) CU of Paul's parents.

Paul (off camera): I have a headache.   (2

188 (=148) CU of Paul. Music.

Paul: Please.   (2

189 (=174) CU of Paul's mother. She looks both thoughtful and apprehensive. Music. Sounds of storm.   (1½

190 (=155) CU of Paul's father. Music. Sound of storm.   (1

191 (=181) CU of doctor. Music. Sound of storm.   (2½

192 (=148) CU of Paul. Music. Sound of storm.   (2

193 (=135) ECU of Paul's eyes. Music. Sound of storm.

                                                       (1½

194   (=151) MS of fireplace. Music. Sound of storm.   (2

195   (=135) ECU of Paul's eyes looking down at fireplace.
      Music. Sound of storm.   (2

196   CU (as seen from left) of Paul's eyes and nose. He looks
      up at ceiling. Music. Sound of storm.   (1½

197   (=196, but as seen from the right) Music. Sound of
      storm.   (1

198   (=135) ECU of Paul's eyes, staring straight ahead.
      Music. Sound of storm.   (1

199   (=196) Music. Sound of storm.   (1

200   (=197) Music. Sound of storm.   (½

201   (=196) Music. Sound of storm.   (¾

202   (=148) CU of Paul turning his head to the right. Music.
      Sound of storm.   (1

203   (=164) MS of Paul, his parents, and the doctor. Paul
      looks at the doctor and his parents, turns abruptly away
      from them, and darts off camera. Camera remains focused
      on his parents and the doctor. Music. Sound of storm.   (1

204   MS of Paul running out of the living room toward the
      camera and past. Low-angle diagonal with Paul up the
      stairs. (Much of shots 204–207 is out of focus.) Music.
      Sound of storm.   (3½

205   CU of stairs and bannister. Diagonal with Paul as he runs
      up the stairs. Music. Sound of storm.   (2

206   MS (low-angle diagonal) of Paul running up the stairs.
      Shot ends on white ceiling. Music. Sound of storm.   (1

207   MS from high angle (top of stairs) of Paul running up
      the stairs. Pan right with Paul, who is in CU at top of
      stairs. He runs past camera to his bedroom door. Music.
      Sound of storm.   (3½

208 MS from high angle of his bedroom door. Screen is very dark. As the door opens, Paul's head becomes visible. Light from window brightens the whole room, though it is not possible to distinguish individual objects. Music. Sound of storm. Storm louder. (2½

209 CU from low angle of Paul, who is illuminated against a dark background. He looks up and then stares intently across the room. Music. Sound of storm. (3

210 MS of Paul's partly opened window, through which illuminated snow gusts into the room. Music. Sound of storm. (4½

211 MS of Paul's bedroom floor, which is being covered with snow. Music. Sound of storm. (4½

212 LS of a model of a sailing ship and a conch shell, which are being covered with snow. Medium pan. Music. Sound of storm. (2½

213 (=209) Paul looks up with beatific expression. Music. Sound of storm. (¾

214 MS from low angle of a globe in Paul's room. The snow continues to fall. Music. Sound of storm. (3½

215 MS of Paul's desk with its books, paper, and pen. Vertical track. Music. Sound of storm.

   Narrator (as voice of the snow): "Listen to us, (5

216 CU of a clipboard, paper, and pen; they, too, are covered with snow. The paper is blown by the wind. Pan left. Music. Sound of storm.

   Narrator: Paul, listen. We have come to tell you the story we told you about. You remember? (11½

217 CU (slightly out of focus) of Paul (as seen from the side) lying in bed, bathed in bright light, raising himself. Music. Sound of storm. (½

218   (=217)   (½

219   (begins near end of shot 217) CU of Paul (as seen from
      the front) raising himself to a sitting position in bed.
      Music. Sound of storm.

            Narrator: In this   (1

220   CU of Paul in profile continuing the motion at end of
      shot 219. He sits up and blinks his eyes. Music. Sound of
      storm.

            Narrator: white darkness, we   (2½

221   CU. Paul looks intently up and around as if he heard
      voices and couldn't see the speakers. His head is turned
      toward the ceiling. He twists his head from side to side.
      Music. Sound of storm.

            Narrator: will take the place of everything."   (8½

222   CU from behind Paul. His arms are raised over his head.
      Music. Sound of storm.   (1

223   CU. Front view of Paul with raised arms and upturned
      face. He smiles. Music. Sound of storm.   (3½

224   (=210) MS of Paul's partly opened window. Music.
      Sound of storm.   (2

225   MCU of Paul. Darkened room. The door is opened,
      slowly revealing Paul and lighting the room. Paul turns
      to light from the door and becomes frightened. Zoom in
      to CU of Paul. There is a look of disbelief on his face.   (4

226   (The same as shots 210 and 224, except that there is no
      snow.)   2

227   MS (low angle, out of focus) of Paul's mother in
      shadows as she is framed in the lighted doorway.   (1½

228   (The same as the end of shot 225.) CU of Paul.   (1½

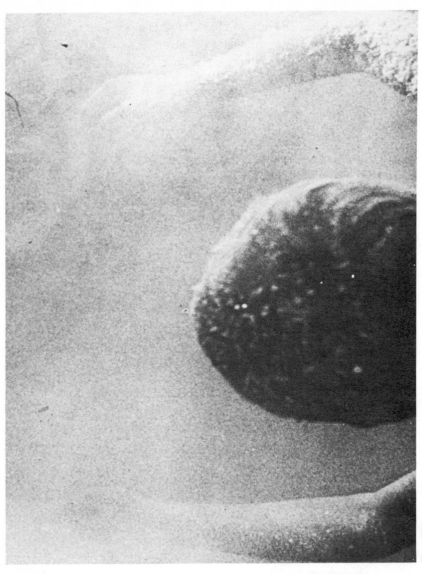

Shot 222.

229   MS of Paul from behind. His bedroom is dark except for
       the lighted doorway, which frames his mother, who is a
       dark, shadowy figure. Paul throws himself back on his
       bed and looks away from his mother. She moves to Paul's
       bed, and as she kneels by his bedside, we can see her face
       clearly.

       Mother: Paul.

       Paul does not answer. He looks tense and nervous. She
       shakes Paul twice as if to wake him.

       Mother (more insistently and loudly—she is almost
       pleading with him): Paul. Paul!   (10½

230   CU (out of focus) of the white sheets on Paul's bed.
       Zip diagonal to CU of Paul's mother.

       Mother (desperately): Paul!   (2

231   (Same as the end of shot 229.) Paul tears away from his
       mother, whose right arm is extended toward him.

       Paul: Go away.

       She looks in a state of anguish and fear. She tries to make
       contact with him.

       Mother (whining pathetically): Paul!

       He again repulses her.

       Paul (harshly and yet hesitantly): I hate you!

            Narrator: And with that effort

       Music.   (8

232   (=210) MS of Paul's partly opened window with snow
       gusting in. Music.

            Narrator: the seamless hiss advanced once more.
            "Listen," it said.   (6

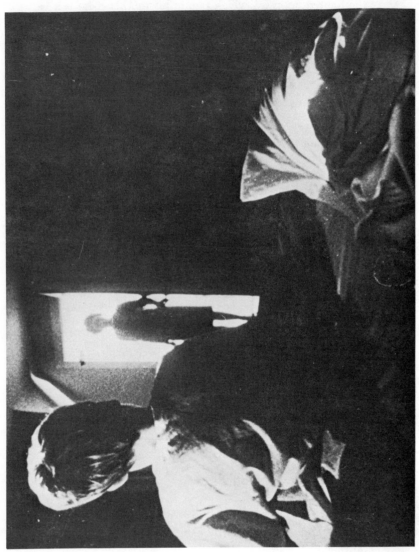

Shot 229.

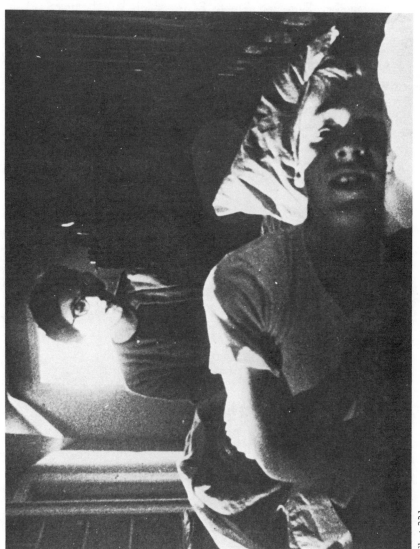

Shot 231.

233   CU of Paul lying on his bed and looking away from his
mother. Slow zoom in to ECU. As his face becomes
blurred and out of focus, a dark shadow moves across the
frame and gradually engulfs it in blackness. Music.

> Narrator (as voice of snow): "We'll tell you the last,
> the most beautiful and secret story, a story that gets
> smaller and smaller, that comes inward instead of
> opening like a flower. It is a flower that becomes a
> seed, a little cold seed, do you hear? We are lean-
> ing closer to you. . . ."   (29

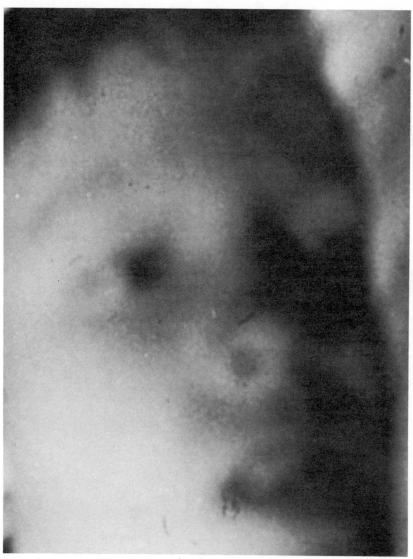

Shot 233.

CRITICISM OF THE FILM

MARTIN A. GARDNER

"Silent Snow,
Secret Snow"
A Chiaroscuro Fantasy

In Gene Kearney's film adaptation of Conrad Aiken's story, "Silent Snow, Secret Snow," there is a major theme often endemic to childhood: fantasy based on the wish to escape from reality. But there is a difference. In this film, Kearney shows us the subtle metamorphosis from mere fantasy to serious psychotic behavior.

The film is the story of Paul, a pre-adolescent who fantasizes about a world covered with the clean soundlessness of snow. Paul's fantasy builds in intensity so that by the end of the film one sees the transformation of Paul into a person for whom fantasy is reality. This transformation is accomplished cinematically by Kearney as he manipulates the mise-en-scenes with a series of jump cuts to finally build to a climax reflecting the emotions of fear, uncertainty, and ignorance, overshadowed by and painted in Gothic grey.

Kearney's camera works smoothly, symbolically. The opening frame is shot almost straight up from the ground and shows the bareness of tree branches outlined in the winter-grey sky. A haunting musical background supports this opening visual, and the credits, in toto, underlining, emphasizing, and setting a mood for mystery. (At one point there is a "jump" in the music, the result of either a bad print or of a neophyte editor who erred in editing the sound film by cutting it as a silent. There also remains the

Martin A. Gardner holds a Ph.D. in film from New York University. He is presently working as a free-lance writer and advertising copywriter. His past professional experience includes work in theater, radio, and television.

possibility that this faux pas is part of careful calculation by Kearney himself, an attempt to create an unsettled mood, as in the purposely annoying shot in On the Beach when the sun comes glaring over Gregory Peck's left shoulder to blast in to the corneas of all in the audience.)

The opening shot of the film (immediately following the credits) is shot through a distorter—somewhat like the fisheye shot often used in still photography to encapsulate the entire geographic boundaries of a locale, such as the popular Life magazine photographs of all of Manhattan's skyscrapers seen in one mind-blowing confusion. Contrasted with this visual distortion is the dulcet enunciation of Michael Keene, voice-over. The oblique narrative (Aiken uses the same technique in the short story) is meant to build suspense, and to create an air of mystery, with Gothic overtones. Next, there is a hard-cut flashback to a classroom, where Kearney's first foreshadowing enters the visual narration, as the school teacher asks a girl student if she can give the geographic definition of the word "equator." When the girl suggests that it is "a line around the middle of the earth," the teacher embarrasses her, sarcastically and ironically, by taking the girl's definition literally to illustrate her lack of verbal precision. She makes her point by suggesting to the girl that she would have been more precise if she had defined the equator as "an imaginary line." The teacher continues with the geography lesson by lecturing about the Arctic Circle (another imaginary line!) and referring to it as a zone of "perpetual snow." These references to imagination and snow not only function as literary foreshadowing but also serve to introduce Paul, medium close-up.

Let us forget the literary foreshadowing for a moment. It is plasticity that allows Kearney to manipulate our emotions and reactions. This plasticity allows Kearney to build a montage leading us toward the conclusions he (and Aiken) wants us to draw. We see Paul awaken in his own bed (and thus, gain an impressionistic view of the change of nature). For Paul has "discovered" that there is snow on the ground, not by seeing it, but by the fact that he has not heard the footsteps of the mailman approaching. It is the suspension of routine that often alerts us to change. We are able to tell by a change in the sound of the familiar that something has altered life as we have been experiencing it (anybody had a blowout lately?). Plasticity, again. Intercuts between Paul in his bed and the mailman's feet help to build to the dramatic climax of the scene. We see the shocking climax in reality: there is no snow. Even more shocking, when Paul discovers that his aural experiences have led to conclusions that appear, in reality, to be untrue, he is not shocked. Or surprised. When he looks out his window and does not see snow, he is only stoic. More, he is happy about his schizophrenic second "life." Back to the literary, again. Paul's discovery and attitude are symbolic clues that perhaps he is not at all happy in the world as most of us know it and that he wants to escape to a world that is covered with snow "muffling the world, hiding the ugly, and deadening increasingly—above all—the steps of the postman." Film, with its plastic ability to jump cut from one visual experience to another, is able to dramatically build this schism between what is perceived in reality and what is perceived in fantasy. In the real world, when fantasy is a substitute for reality, these schisms can create mental disturbance.

Kearney gradually takes us into Paul's withdrawal into schizophrenia. Visually he shows us fragments of physical reality: a child's hand waving in mid air trying to get teacher's attention, mailman's feet walking, gargoyles and griffins atop a stone wall, a shot of Paul looking out from his bedroom window with the sun forming a white-out on half the window. Kearney contrasts these elements of reality with fantasy by using them in jump-cut flashbacks, so that there is a transfer from film reality to film fantasy. It is with the technique of plasticity that Kearney is able to create a sense of Paul's disturbed outlook.

Plasticity is one of the arts of film, and it is an art which Kearney uses to its utmost. The flashback and jump cut in a film can compress time and space and motion much more quickly and efficiently than the same technique in a short story or novel. Aiken uses the technique in the short story. But basically it is a film technique because it can be performed instantly.

Kearney also uses a tracking shot to extend time and help build psychological suspense. As Paul returns home from school, Kearney shows us the "items of mere externality" on the way, trucking the camera along so that we see, in a Paul's-eye view, the Gothic statues sitting on a wall. This augments Paul's inner thoughts to help build suspense for us. (It might be interesting to note that at this point as I was watching the film, my secretary entered, and watching it for a few minutes, asked me if Paul was, in effect, dead. She had perceived the mood of the entire film within a few minutes of watching a fragment, and without any of the preliminary build-up.)

And when Paul finally comes to Hill Street, he discovers the reality of barrenness. But from Paul's eye, from the subjective camera, the street is covered with snow. From the objective camera eye, we see no snow. It is here that Kearney has presented with ultimate simplicity, impressionistic fantasy. There is no need to set up an optical ellipsis. The camera can be elliptical just by recording the disparity between fantasy and reality. And so Kearney has done it that simply, with a direct technique that is basic and spare. He uses a hard cut rather than a tricky optical effect to bring us to the suddenness of schizophrenia. This is the way dreams are perceived: fantasy arrives at the blink of an eye, not in gradual smoke-and-thunder-framed sequences, or gelatinous opticals (see *The Pawnbroker*). The theatricality of optical effects, when depicting fantasy, divorces us from the realities of fear and shock. If Paul's fantasies were staged in this theatrical manner, we might laugh at them. Instead, Kearney's depiction of the psychological manifestations of fear and fantasy brings them to us in the problematical way, not the theatrical. Thus, the dream sequences—the excursions into fantasy—leave doubts in the viewer's mind. And this is one of the objects of Kearney's film: to create an impressionistic, complex, psychological study. In real life, schizophrenia does leave doubts. Events for the schizophrenic are elliptical. He cannot definitively tell the difference between real events and imagined events. Paul doesn't know. And, we don't either (as my secretary didn't quite know). The intensity of Paul's imagined world broadens as the film continues. More and more his dream world overtakes his sense of "reality" so that fantasy becomes reality for him.

Kearney strengthens the sense of fantasy in the film with a rather interesting aural technique when he lets the voice-over become omnipresent in Paul's thoughts. The voice-over becomes Paul's "inner voices"—that is, the snow beckoning him—rather than just the voice of narration. The voice has become Paul's mind just as frequently real-life schizophrenics complain of hearing "voices."

As in the earlier sequence when Paul "discovers" his secret snow, Kearney builds to a final climax with elements of fantasy and symbolic techniques to help him. Kearney paints a chiaroscuro picture to help build the suspense of the final scenes. He stages the doctor's examination scene—the "inquisition"—in shades of black and white and brown and grey and dark shadows and angles and harsh lights. The doctor and Paul's parents are made to appear ugly. The simplest of their questions seems to be loaded with implied accusation. This "inquisition" builds to a frenzy in Paul's mind, causing him to flee to his room; his private world. The ambiguous climax occurs in Paul's room as we see the snow whirling and cascading around him. He crosses the line from our world to his with his rejection of his mother, who has followed him to offer help and comfort. Kearney shows the culmination of Paul's slide-over to his "secret" world when we see him sitting up in bed to greet the "snow" which has entered his room. Kearney repeats the shot of Paul rising up from a supine position, thus extending its effect and subsequently implanting it in our consciousness with its suspension of reality. Kearney has used this cinematic technique in its exact sense: the ambiguity of the scene becomes the ambiguity of the film, and thus we are able to draw final conclusions about Paul after seeing this final, numbing climax. At last we can assemble the jagged pieces of Paul's world.

I must confess that upon first viewing the film, I did not like it. I was angry with it. Why? Because here we see a beautiful depiction of a psychologically disturbed person on the brink of complete transference from normality to schizophrenia, and yet we do not know why. Paul wants to escape from the bleak, grey world around him. Yet there seems to be no outer (or inner) reasons for his alienation and conflict. He lives in a comfortable, middle class home on a nice street. His parents are not ogres: they don't chain him to his bed or beat him or starve him or deprive him. As a matter of fact, they're rather sensitive to his feelings, offering to investigate, rather intelligently, his alienation. His schoolroom seems to present no problems; his teacher does not seem to be a monster.

We see no scenes of peer-group rivalry or taunting. So, at first, I was confused. My first reaction to the film was in the form of questions. Why is Paul trying to escape? From what is he trying to escape?

The usual manifestation of escape occurs after an upsetting experience in which the child envisions himself dead, with crowds of all those who have "wronged" him surrounding his coffin, himself included (in order to gulp down gallons of self-pity). However, the fact remains that we see nothing happen to Paul to upset him and cause him to want to escape from a horrible world.

It wasn't until the second or third viewing that the raison d'etre of Kearney's film began to dawn on me. "Silent Snow, Secret Snow" is a study of the precise moment in a person's life when he is on the brink of slipping over to a serious psychological disturbance. Paul is treading the line of schizophrenia: a delicate balance between two worlds, his white, comfortable, cold "snow" world, and the black, grim, grey world of external reality. The causes do not matter. The moment of change is important, for it is a moment we rarely see in a person's life. And it is this moment we are seeing here.

Certainly Aiken's short story gives us no clues. We can accept that in a short story. But in a film it is difficult, because film deals with pictorial reality. We are used to seeing films "explain" the human problems they investigate. We should allow film to create impressionistic studies of human beings and other things. To accept film only on a level of clinical reality is to accept film with delimitations which minimize its possibilities. Kearney has allowed himself to open these possibilities for us. We should see more of the films for impressionistic thought. From this we can gain some self-revelatory insights about the world around us. That's what film is all about. And that's what "Silent Snow, Secret Snow" is all about.

DISCUSSION QUESTIONS

1. Explain what is meant by plasticity in film and describe instances in which meaning is communicated through film plasticity. With respect to literature, do you agree that plasticity "is basically ... a film technique because it can be performed instantly?"

2. Some elements in the film are described as Gothic: the lighting, the narrative speaker, the statues seen during Paul's homeward walk. Look up the meaning of "Gothic" in a literary handbook. In what way could the film be described as Gothic?

3. Gardner suggests that Kearney's use of hard-cut transitions from objective reality to subjective fantasy is more effective than the various optical techniques employed in some films because the hard-cut transitions are more realistic and serve to reinforce theme. Do you agree with this as a generalization that could be applied to all films?

4. In his description of Paul repeatedly rising from his bed during the last scene of the film, Gardner notes that "the ambiguity of the scene becomes the ambiguity of the film." What is meant by this statement? What does it imply about the nature of film art?

5. The essay concludes with a defense of the film as a study of the period when a person is balanced between the world of reality and the world of fantasy. Thus we need not understand the reasons for Paul's condition, for it is the presentation of his condition that is important. Do you agree that the film contains no clues that explain the cause of Paul's condition? Is it true that we tend to accept the lack of such clues in a work of literature but not in a film?

JERRY HERMAN

A Magic World Betrayed: The Failure of "Silent Snow, Secret Snow"

Many filmmakers, from the most commercial to the farthest out of the *avant garde*, have tried to externalize the internal, to show in images what happens in the mind exactly as it occurs. Indeed, the film medium seems uniquely suited for this kind of re-creation, since it can portray both visual and audial images directly as well as treat time and space more flexibly than any other man-developed medium we now know. Language has a different sort of flexibility and many more limitations than film has, but one reason many believe language to be a superior medium to film is simply that language has been around so long that man has developed it into an extraordinarily sophisticated and complex instrument. Moving pictures have been with us for less than a century. Imagine the medium after 1000 years!

Gene Kearney, who made the film "Silent Snow, Secret Snow," took up this task of externalizing the internal and failed in his attempt to show effectively the inner workings of the mind of a young boy who is sinking into a total psychological withdrawal from the world. To portray the evolution of this condition by trying to depict thoughts and images in the mind is immensely difficult, but other filmmakers have posed comparable problems for themselves and have succeeded brilliantly. Several films come to mind immediately: *The Cabinet of Dr. Caligari*, Ingmar Bergman's

Jerry Herman teaches English at Laney College, where he is chairman of the department. Currently he is compiling an anthology of personal experience writing entitled *A Time of Their Lives*.

163

Wild Strawberries, and Federico Fellini's 8½. There are others—
but not many.

Although film is better suited to portray inner reality than any
other medium yet developed, its capabilities for reproducing inner
states have hardly been tapped, largely because film is even better
suited to re-create external reality, the physical world around us,
and most of the conventions in filmmaking have stressed over-
whelmingly a faithful reproduction of the world we see with our
eyes rather than the ones we see behind them.

Dreams are a good example. We all know that the logic, co-
herence, and time sequence in dreams is usually quite different
from that of waking reality, yet it has been standard for filmmakers to simply hang out a cinematic sign saying that a character is
dreaming (medium shot of person sleeping or dozing off; zoom in
to his eyes and go out of focus; the next scene will portray his
dream) and proceed to make that dream appear very much like
waking reality. The average filmgoer has accepted this convention,
and even sophisticated viewers and critics rarely protest it.

One reason that language has been successful in relating inner
states is that it cannot reproduce but only suggest. Words are not
the natural medium for the working mind, but they do trigger
images and ideas which would not have occurred without them;
hence the power of metaphor and the consequent value of poetry
specifically and literature in general. In other words, the mind receives images and ideas, fashions a script, and makes an instantane-
ous movie of its own, in its own way. An example of the way
this works is pre-television radio which presented drama, situation
comedies, sports, and so forth. Many people still feel that radio in
those days was a more interesting medium than is television because one could "use his imagination" to visualize characters, situations, and settings. The advent of television brought into people's
living rooms "the real thing," which many with vivid imaginations
thought to be only a drab version of the images their minds could
create from the radio script.

One of the major failures of "Silent Snow, Secret Snow" is
Kearney's use of a narrative which is highly suggestive simultane-
ously with visual images which are, for the most part, mundane.
In short, the movie that my mind was stimulated to make as I

listened to the narrative was far superior to the one Kearney was able to fabricate. If this flies in the face of the theory that visual stimulation in films is more powerful than the words spoken, then so be it.

The film's chief character, the young boy Paul, is drifting from a hostile external world into one which is the creation of his own mind, a world in which all will eventually be engulfed in the white darkness of a silent snow isolating him from everything outside of himself. This is a completely seductive idea to him, not a terrifying one, and he greets each step in the evolution of his condition with hope and delight. To create a metaphor for his withdrawal as perfect and archetypal as being buried in snow, Paul works at a potent level of imagination, regardless of the pathology of his state. We *hear* all of this, and it is eloquent. But as Kearney attempts to present visually the inner process of this fascinating and pathetic imagination, the best he can come up with is some shots of the sky through barren trees and a three-inch snow fall on Paul's street that has been driven and trodden on. Are we to believe that *this* is the incredibly seductive lure that Paul has created in his imagination? Are these pedestrian visual images powerful enough to match the wonderland of secret, silent snow which Paul's psyche has chosen over a world of hostile teachers, parents and doctors? As Paul thinks of the magnificence of the North Pole (a fascinating place for most of us, too; we have even established it as Santa's home), the viewer sees last night's frozen precipitation, predicted by the local weather board, soon to be removed by municipal snowplows.

It seems that Kearney has been seduced by the great convention of reproducing external reality. The snow of Paul's imagination is as much the snow that the weather bureau predicts and records as Santa Claus' reindeer are the ones you can find at your local zoo. Either Kearney failed to recognize this, in which case he made a glaring error in his conception of the film, or he did not have the resources at his disposal to present more than dull external reality, in which case he should not have made the film. Whatever the case, he has not satisfactorily portrayed Paul's inner world.

Perhaps a major error in judgment on Kearney's part was his choice of having a narrative at all. It is possible to imagine the film without narration although this presents greater difficulty to the filmmaker. I believe, however, that the greater difficulty would have forced a more creative approach than simply an attempt to supply literal images for a highly charged narrative. One can contrast Kearney's film with Roberto Enrico's film version of "An Occurrence at Owl Creek Bridge." In that film Enrico also delves into the mind of an individual, although the audience is led to believe that it is watching external reality rather than a man's fantasy flashing in an instant before him. Yet the whole film is done virtually without dialogue or narration. Toward the end of the film, when the chief character seems to have escaped from his pursuers to home, wife, and safety, Enrico repeats four or five times a shot of him running, giving the audience a stunning sense that time has been suspended, that the man will never reach his wife's outstretched arms, as indeed he never really does. That sequence, startling in its effectiveness, is an accurate reproduction of an inner state. When the narrator in "Silent Snow, Secret Snow" says that Paul's walking home from school seems timeless, we get no effective visual sense of that at all. If we believe in that timelessness it is because we have heard it, not because we have seen it.

The stone-faced boy who plays Paul apparently was directed to maintain a far-off look in his eye, which is at times appropriate, but at other times, ridiculous. If we are privy to Paul's inner world and hear about his bliss at the oncoming snow, then we should see some visual manifastation of that bliss or the agony that is causing him to withdraw, but, alas, we get none of that. Worlds which seem either hostile or attractive to him look uniformly dull and mundane to us.

The characters he seems to resent—mailman, mother, father, teacher, doctor—do not have to be presented as monsters, but at least there should be some clue as to Paul's feelings toward them. A central problem here lies in the bad acting of those who play the adult roles. When Paul's father says, "How is school going, son? History was my favorite subject," I cringed with embarrassment at both the falsity of the line and the ineptness of its delivery. The obvious contrast between the professional ability of the narrator and the strident awkwardness of the actors who speak the dialogue also serves to diminish the effect of the film.

In general Kearney seems to have missed the opportunities and challenges which "Silent Snow, Secret Snow" presented. One of the only reasons for making such a film, outside of its value as a psychological case study, is so that its audience may recognize that beyond the external reality which is so painful to Paul there is a magic world which, from some compelling psychological need, he has created for himself. His world is not our world, his pain is not our pain, his magic is not our magic; but one of the functions of art is that it can allow its audience to share in a meaningful way the experiences, even the most private experiences, of others, and thereby recognize the common thread that holds mankind together. Kearney's opportunity in "Silent Snow, Secret Snow" was to create for his audience a world as magical as Paul's secret world if not one as painful as the external world was for him. Instead of taking advantage of this opportunity, Kearney created a lackluster world in which neither pain nor joy holds a significant place.

DISCUSSION QUESTIONS

1. Herman believes that a major failure of the film is that the "highly suggestive" language of the narrator is superior to the "mundane" images that are simultaneously presented. What is the implicit criterion behind this view? Is it in conflict with the generally held theory that the visual image tends to take precedence over the spoken word in a film? Do you think that the relationship between word and image in the film is a major failure?

2. Paul is described as "drifting from a hostile external world." What evidence in the film supports this view? Later in the essay, we are told that Kearney gives us no clues that would help us to understand Paul's feelings toward the adults. Are these statements contradictory?

3. It is suggested that Kearney's scenes of snow are "pedestrian" and do not give us a satisfactory vision of Paul's inner state. What could the director have done

to present a more explicit feeling of Paul's inner world? Would such changes add or detract from the meaning of the film?

4. The poor acting of the adults is contrasted to the professional abilities of the narrator. Is this apparent contrast the result of poor acting or poor directing? Why might the director have had the parts played in a particular way?

5. Herman suggests that the film could have been made without a narrator. How could this have been done? Would the resulting film differ noticeably from Kearney's film with respect to theme and tone?

LEE R. BOBKER

"Silent Snow,
Secret Snow"

The art of the motion picture is primarily a "narrative" or story telling art. In this respect, it is, of course, related to the novel, the short story, and the theatre. Until the early 1940s, film was used in a standard dramatic fashion—words and pictures enacting story. However, one of the key elements that served to separate cinema from its sister arts was its ability to transmit internal emotions, thoughts and ideas—not readily visible on the stage—through elliptical images and the creative use of fantasy images that evoked in the minds of the audience the unseen. Thus, when a filmmaker seeks to create a work that deals largely with the unseen and unspoken, the character and quality of his sounds and images must carry a very large burden.

A contemporary film such as Z is purely narrative exposition—telling a direct story and dealing only with the events in that story. On the opposite end of the film scale is *Easy Rider*, which intersperses its narrative events with highly evocative, unreal images designed to project the internal life and world of its principals (for example the New Orleans graveyard sequence).

The short film "Silent Snow, Secret Snow," based on a brilliant short story by Conrad Aiken, is a motion picture designed solely around the *internal* life of its principal character. The actual dramatic events in the film are minor and of little importance.

The basic "story" deals with an interior view of a solitary, intro-

Lee R. Bobker is one of the country's leading documentary filmmakers. He has been given over 200 awards for his work and has been nominated for an Academy Award on three occasions. He has taught courses on the contemporary cinema and has written a book on the subject, *Elements of Film.*

169

verted child caught in the process of withdrawal from the real world. The film itself is structured around (1) a narrative voice reading selected sections of the original short story, (2) spoken dialogue enacting illustrative episodes with action, (3) a combination of real and fantasy visual images supporting the spoken text. Because so much of the story remains half hidden in the disturbed mind of the child, the film runs into difficulties almost immediately.

The filmmakers have elected at the outset to freely alternate between hard, real images of the boy's external life (school, home, family) and poetic fantasy images illustrating his *inner* life. Unfortunately, the camera and lighting styles fail to clearly differentiate these two worlds and the performances are just not good enough to project the view within the child. Very rarely in film have actors been able to project madness unless it is of the teethgnashing, rock-throwing, tantrum variety. The boy in "Silent Snow, Secret Snow" can only sit and stare, seeking to look melancholy and disturbed. Unfortunately, he seems only retarded or distracted.

In the early scenes, we see the boy in school beginning to divide his attention between the real world and the growing fantasy world into which he is retreating. The sense of the classroom carried by the live dialogue and the flat, straight images is fine—standard, relatively uninteresting, but correct for the purpose. After all, this is the reality from which the boy is fleeing. The problem, however, is the filmmaker's lack of imagination when he seeks to communicate so early in the film the *fact* of the boy's retreat. The child sits in the classroom, we hear what he hears, see what he sees—but when his fantasy world begins to intrude, we see only a vacant stare and we hear only the narrator reading the words from the short story, "*telling*" us what he feels. This is not film—it is photographing a short story . . . quite a different thing.

The audience, then, is asked to divide its attention between what is seen and what is heard. The point of view (visually) is changed abruptly. Where we have been seeing and listening to the reality from the boy's viewpoint, we now are asked to view the child from the viewpoint of his teacher and his classmates, to whom he looks simply inattentive, moody, and a little strange. Thus we are "seeing" from one viewpoint and being "told" from another. It just doesn't work. The burden placed on the child actor is too great, and we get no real vision of the nature of the problem upon which the film depends.

A good contrast for the film student would be to study Max von Sydow's performance in *Hour of the Wolf* where this kind of inner withdrawal was successfully suggested by a master actor.

Thus, in "Silent Snow, Secret Snow," since neither camera nor performance successfully delineates the nature of this inner world so steadily enveloping the child, we are left to rely on the narration. This type of spoken narration defies visualization.

> "The thing was above all a secret, something to be preciously concealed from Mother and Father; and to that very fact it owed an enormous part of its deliciousness."

Throughout the film, we are harassed by the same problem—the narration, telling us of the child's feelings which are dark and deep and incredibly melancholy, simply cannot be supported by visual images of a child lying in bed unless the extreme close up view of the child's face tells us something of the nature of the problem. This is very difficult to do . . . even for the best of actors.

A detailed examination of the *elements of film* employed in "Silent Snow, Secret Snow" can tell us more about why the film does not succeed.

1. NARRATIVE—*Content and Performance*

A. *Content*

A film narrative, if it is to have any value at all, must be written so as to support the visual material and not lead or overwhelm it. A good example of spoken narration that enriches a film is that of the opening minutes of Resnais' *Hiroshima, Mon Amour*. In "Silent Snow, Secret Snow," the words are sometimes visualized on a didactic one-to-one basis, as in the following section:

> But on this particular morning, the first morning, as *he lay there with his eyes closed*, he had for some reason waited for the postman. He wanted to hear him come

round the corner. And that was precisely the joke—he never did. He never came. He never had come—round the corner—again. For when at last the steps were heard, they had already, he was quite sure, *come a little down the hill*, to the first house; and even so, the steps were curiously different—they were softer, they had a new secrecy about them, *they were muffled and indistinct*; and while the *rhythm of them was the same*, it now said a new thing—it said peace, it said remoteness, it said cold, it said sleep. And he had understood the situation at once—nothing could have seemed simpler —there had been snow in the night, such as all winter he had been longing for; and it was this which had rendered the postman's first footsteps inaudible, and the later ones faint. Of course! How lovely! And even now it must be snowing—it was going to be a snowy day— *the long white ragged lines were drifting and sifting across the street*, across the faces of the old houses, whispering and hushing, making little *triangles of white in the corners between cobblestones, seething* a little when *the wind blew them over the ground* to a drifted corner; and so it would be all day, getting deeper and deeper and silenter and silenter.

In this portion of the film, the images and sounds match almost exactly the spoken word. (I have italicized the specific scenes that support this sequence.) Dutifully, the camera gives us shots of the boy lying in his bed in the half-darkened room, he closes his eyes, we see the feet of the postman, we hear the sound— exactly as described—we see standard black and white shots of the street, the snow, and we hear a bit of wind. The problem here is that by simply changing the sound track and substituting, for example, a narrative taken from a travelogue describing a New England town in winter, the images would work as well. This fact reveals the inadequacy of the images because when the image is exactly right, it will not be easily transferrable to other usage. For example, could the scenes accompanying the voice-over narration in the opening of *Hiroshima* work as well with any other narrative? I doubt it. What the above segment of narrative cried out for was *interpretive* images revealing the soft seduction of this beckoning world. So we, the audience, could catch a glimpse of that strange sickness occurring inside the mind of the child. Then the translation of a short story into another form is justified because our perception is heightened and the art of film extends the boundaries of the form in which the original was conceived.

Because this is not done and because the images are simply the photography suggested by the words, one watches not an evocative combination of words and pictures, but direct illustration of the story. The just balance that should exist in film—images supported by sound—is distorted to its exact opposite with a resultant loss of filmic character.

To further confuse the audience, there is little or no consistency to the filmmaker's approach. At times, the words are accompanied by elliptical images designed to evoke their deeper meanings as in this section:

> And the mist of snow, as he had foreseen, was still on it—a *ghost of snow falling in the bright sunlight*, softly and steadily floating and turning and pausing, soundlessly meeting the snow that covered, as with a *transparent mirage*, the bare bright cobbles. *He loved it*—he stood still and loved it. Its beauty was paralyzing—*beyond all words, all experience, all dream*. No fairy story he had ever read could be compared with it—none had ever given him this extraordinary combination of ethereal loveliness with a *something else, unnameable*, which was just faintly and *deliciously terrifying*. What was this thing? As he thought of it, he looked upward toward his own bedroom window, which was open—and it was as if he looked straight into the room and saw himself lying half awake in his bed. There he was —at this very instant he was still perhaps actually there —more truly there than standing here at the edge of the cobbled hill-street, with one hand lifted to shade his eyes against the snow-sun. Had he indeed ever left his room, in all this time? since that very first morning: Was the whole progress still being enacted there, was it still the same morning, and himself not yet wholly awake? And even now, had the postman not yet come round the corner? . . .

This paragraph is supported by shots of snow on trees—snow on the ground—snow falling—all photographed as poetic imagery now accompanying the underlined sections of the narrative. Now the images do not attempt to realistically match the words, but communicate the "sense" of them. Unfortunately, they remain simply pretty shots of snow.

Specifically, the camera does nothing but expose shots . . . and here we come to a very basic problem in filmmaking. The film-maker is not nor ever should be a photographer. The camera is, after all, his paintbrush, paint, and canvas. It is his artistic responsibility to create images—using movement (both within the frame and of the frame itself), for this is the key element that separates film from theatre. He must *design* each frame in terms of light and shadow, composition and motion to communicate the inner values related to the film he is making. Any amateur equipped with a cheap camera and film can shoot pretty shots of snow. But review again the key ideas contained in the narrative designed to evoke the world into which the child is descending: "ghost," "transparent mirage," "loved it" (this is repeated), "paralyzing beauty," "dream," "unnameable," and a superb two-word combination—"deliciously terrifying." Does the camera communicate this? Shut off the sound and try to describe the images yourself—and it is just as easy, indeed, even more likely to come up with "beautiful," "pretty," "pleasant," "cold," "white," and other dull postcard descriptions.

What might have been done is only conjecture. Slow motion dolly shots in the style of Resnais' opening of *Last Year At Marienbad* or *Nuit et Bruillard*, long lens photography in the manner of Widerberg's *Elvira Madigan*, the dream distortion of the wide angle lens as used by Bergman (Fischer) in *Wild Strawberries*, or the extreme unnatural and seductive use of menacing shadows as used by Fellini in *8½* or Nyquist in *Hour of the Wolf*. Dreams and nightmare worlds have always fascinated the filmmaker because they are ideally suited to his art. It is useful to analyze such work as the opening nightmare in *8½* (the traffic jam)—the fantasies in *Julietta of the Spirits* by Fellini—and the work of Bergman in *Through A Glass Darkly, Wild Strawberries*, and *Hour of the Wolf* to see what can be achieved through lens and light in black and white photography.

It remains then to be said that "Silent Snow, Secret Snow" fails to give us images that evoke an insight into this inner world. The images are ordinary and so the film depends on the spoken word to make its point, and the viewer listens and does not really understand.

B. Performance

The actor-narrator (Michael Keene, I believe) is intelligent and does a professional, workman-like job. When he is at his best (the blander sections where the beauty of the language commands its own attention), the sound of his voice draws us away from the images, and when he is at his weakest (the end of the film when he assumes an actor's dramatic interpretation), he distracts us so the images (the snow falling in the room) seem ludicrous.

2. CAMERA AND LIGHTING

Because the material cries out for a highly original and creative camera style, it is this element that is the most disappointing. The realistic scenes (classroom, home, doctor's examination) are in the worst tradition of the 1930s Hollywood films. Heavy, false shadows, exaggerated clarity, immobility of the camera itself, self-conscious compositions . . . all calling attention to the "art" of film. The fantasy scenes (as indicated earlier) demanding the kind of visual art we see in Widerberg's *Elvira Madigan*, or Hopper's *Easy Rider* just don't succeed. A few of the snow scenes are pretty, looking a bit like a good Gregg Toland film circa 1940 (*Citizen Kane*), or a bad Conrad Hall film of 1969 (*Butch Cassidy and the Sundance Kid*).

The sound track is telling us that the snow is a symbol of a quiet place where Paul can be safe, where he can hide and sleep, where he can escape from "the hostile presences," but the images on screen are showing cold, white, wet snow. Here is where the film could have succeeded, for the visual image is far more capable of suggesting other worlds than is the spoken word, but here the filmmaker's imagination failed him and us. Compare these semi-realistic static and earthbound scenes with the New Orleans graveyard sequence in *Easy Rider* and we can begin to suspect what might have been possible with this material.

3. EDITING AND SOUND

Again, a totally conventional job has been done. Match-ups of picture and narration on a one-to-one basis (the postman sequence), dissolves, matched action cuts, and metric dialogue editing just as we were doing when Hollywood was in its glory. The editing in this film is identical with a film like *Now Voyageur*, a Bette Davis classic—narration matches picture and dialogue is cut on beats. There is literally no creative overlapping of sound and not a single instance of counterpoint between picture and sound. For example, what might have been the result of matching up the dialogue contained in the scene where the boy's mother badgers him for some explanation of his behavior with truly creative images of his new world? The contrast might have given us some insight into the dynamics of what is going on inside his mind. The single most creative use of sound in many years is found in the black comedy *M.A.S.H.* and is worth studying for this alone. In 1940 *Citizen Kane* used sound and editing far more creatively than "Silent Snow, Secret Snow" uses it. Unfortunately, this film demands something else of the editor. A different pacing, perhaps, direct cuts as in *They Shoot Horses, Don't They?*, as opposed to obvious dissolves. Remember that von Sydow's inner hallucinations in *Hour of the Wolf* were revealed by direct cuts and the audience was propelled within the delusion. If this story had any initial chance of success, the entire artistic approach on film would have had to be far more unconventional.

4. MUSIC

George Kleinsinger's score, although conventional and not terribly interesting, is probably the most successful element in the film. The editorial decision to begin and end the music concurrently with the narrative does evoke a mood consistent with the material and the cello, as always, is quite effective in conjuring up the schizophrenic world into which Paul descends. (Review Bergman's use of the Bach Cello Suite in B in *Through A Glass Darkly*, used for exactly the same purpose.)

The sound effects, however, of the wind and snow are a disastrous mistake, adding a note of reality to the "silent" fantasy world Paul embraces. The words in the title "Silent," "Secret" should have cued the filmmaker's decision on sound effects. The sound of the postman's footsteps are well used because they fit the narrative and heighten the mounting terror.

5. DIRECTION

I have left a discussion of the over-all direction of the film until the end because here, of course, must lie the blame or the credit, and here, it seems to me, is the source of the film's failure. It is the director's responsibility to control every element of the film and so the previous discussion of the failure of the camera, sound, and editing must fall here. The choice of the actors is also his and the actors are just terrible. They are unable to deliver even the simplest of lines and the director does nothing to help. Frozen faces staring, looking, dreaming do not (despite Gregory Peck's success) communicate worry, depth, concern, anger, or anything else. Despite the honesty of approach, there is no style, no central approach, no single cinematic concept that might have elevated the film.

At the end of the film, the director has made his most serious mistake. The boy has now retreated to his room and instead of relying on the words of the story as the boy lies in his bed, we are treated to a science fiction image of snow falling within the room to realistically visualize the boy's internal fantasy. Paul does not *think* he actually sees snow in his room—he *feels* the comfort and the warmth and the silence of what the white snow symbolizes for him. The director's choice here works against the film and misleads the audience and breaks the mood.

Thus, we can see the great dangers of being *too* filmic. Because film can visualize is no reason that it should. The comfort offered by the feeling of the snow is obviated by the sight of the cold, windy snow filling his room. He would scarcely embrace this "snow ghost." Compounding the problem, the director now elects to have the narrator dramatize the voice of the snow, whispering beguiling words à la Schubert's *Erlkoenig*.

> "Listen to us!" it said. "Listen! We have come to tell you the story we told you about. You remember? Lie down. Shut your eyes, now—you will no longer see much—in this white darkness who could see, or want to see? We will take the place of everything . . . Listen—"

The voice cannot match the one we ourselves can evoke and thus, it all becomes a nightmare, a little boy's fear of the dark, instead of a final surrender to madness.

Again, it would be tremendously useful to analyze a key sequence from *Hour of the Wolf*. When the artist is transported with a full blown schizophrenic fantasy of an erotic nature seeing a former lover, naked on a coffin, every element is used to clearly indicate (1) that we are watching something going on internally and (2) why the artist chooses this particular kind of fantasy. Heavy, subtle shadows—highly exaggerated, combine with wide angle lens to so distort the image that it could not be real, and yet there is a comfort and sexual warmth in the translucent body of the woman. This is offset by the terrible fear created by the symbols of Death. We then understand the conflict destroying the artist. He seeks love and comfort and finds it only in Death which, like all of us, he fears. We then share his trauma—and we understand. The final scenes of "Silent Snow, Secret Snow" are the moment when Paul rushes over, gives himself up to his "other world" and the film fails to make us understand the attraction this world holds for this boy. The room is cold—the snow not beguiling, but threatening. One is tempted to say simply—"get up and close the window."

Here, no camera, lighting, editing, music could have given us a look behind the curtain—soft focus, gentle shadows, *unseen snow*, flash cut subliminal fragments of white on white—receding sounds of mother and father and doctor—and finally, the comfort of silence. Think of the child's retreat in the silent corridors of the great hotel in Bergman's *The Silence*.

To conclude, film is, like all art, the sum total of *all* its parts. Every element must be created to communicate a single central mood or idea. "Silent Snow, Secret Snow" is a simple short story

—designed in the classical sense, to transmit all the factors involved in the moment a child leaves the real world for the comfort of a world of his own creation. The short film, "Silent Snow, Secret Snow," aside from its spoken narrative, does not communicate in any of its parts this central idea.

The artistic range of a mobile and creative camera (*Wild Strawberries*), the subtle relationships between sound and picture, dialogue and narration (*Hiroshima, Mon Amour*), the careful selection and handling of actors capable of communicating inner torment (von Sydow—*Hour of the Wolf*, Anderson—*Through A Glass Darkly*), the contributive contribution of music and sound (*Through A Glass Darkly*), and the complex relationships of picture to picture, sound to sound, and picture to sound in the editing (*Midnight Cowboy,Z*)—all these are missing from "Silent Snow, Secret Snow." As in any film, they are essential for success.

DISCUSSION QUESTIONS

1. "A film narrative . . . must be written so as to support the visual material and not lead or overwhelm it." What evidence is presented to support this view? Is it convincing?

2. "The images are ordinary and so the film depends on the spoken word to make its point, and the viewer listens and does not really *understand* [italics ours]." What are the implications of this statement?

3. Given the evidence of the shot analysis, do the comments on dialogue and editing seem valid to you?

4. The last scene of the film is considered "*too filmic.*" Given the earlier comments concerning the film's lack of "filmic" qualities, is this a contradictory judgment?

5. Summarize Bobker's interpretation of the meaning of the film. Do his criticisms grow out of his interpretation?

GERALD R. BARRETT

A Film Is a Short Story
Is a Film: Gene Kearney's
"Silent Snow,
Secret Snow"

Gene Kearney's film "Silent Snow, Secret Snow" (1966), an adaptation of Conrad Aiken's short story of the same name, serves as an interesting example of the problems involved in attempting to capture on film the spirit of a particular literary genre. When William Faulkner suggested that the short story required "a more absolute exactitude" than the novel and that "almost every word be almost exactly right," he was paraphrasing Poe's famous dictum that every word should reinforce the design of the story. The short story often couples metaphoric compression with an exactitude of diction in order to produce a succinct and suggestive literary work. Stories such as James Joyce's "Araby," Katherine Ann Porter's "Flowering Judas," and Conrad Aiken's "Silent Snow, Secret Snow" exemplify the rich texture and suggestiveness that results, but one wonders whether the medium of film is capable of capturing the spirit of the form as well as the content.

Robert Breer, an experimental filmmaker, made an eleven-minute film, *Fist Fight* (1964), in which every frame is an isolated image. In other words, the film bombards the audience with 15,840 separate images in eleven minutes (at 24 frames per second). Based on what we know about our persistence of vision, the brain "holds" an image for one-tenth of a second. When an object changes slightly from frame to frame, we have the illusion of movement.

However, when each frame is a photograph of a different object, the result is a blur, an impression, a feeling. Suppose each image in Breer's film were to be selected and placed in the film in such a way that the succinctness and metaphoric compression often found in the short story would result. Would the audience be able to make sense of the film? Of course not.

This is a grossly exaggerated example of the problem any film-maker would have in attempting to adapt the *form* of the compressed, highly suggestive short story as well as the *content*. While a reader can pause, think, re-read, and continue, the viewer does not have this luxury; the projector continues to run at 24 frames per second, regardless of the complexities of the material being presented. Even if one assumes multiple viewings of a particular film, the initial viewing experience should be such that the viewer would want to see the film again in order to deepen his under-standing. Any serious filmmaker understands the built-in limitations of his chosen art form and must take them into account as he shapes his finished work.

With respect to "Silent Snow, Secret Snow," one wonders if Kearney was conscious of the risks he was taking; while the film contains many interesting, visually expressed ideas, this may only become apparent and understandable after a number of showings. Prior to that time, one may have the feeling that the language of the narrator dominates the meaning of the film to the extent that the visuals can often be seen as rather neutral backdrops off of which the words reverberate. In reality, Kearney has developed a complex system of visual images that give us clues to the cause of the protagonist's state, as well as suggest his inner condition. While the narrator is describing Paul, patterns of visual images suggest his world. In this essay, I want to explain this interpreta-tion, an interpretation derived from viewing the film a number of times. Since the reader may want to check the evidence presented, specific reference will be made to the shot analysis.

The film begins with a fade-in on a large tree that dominates the right side of the frame. The rest of the frame is filled with a network of branches set against a darkened sky. The opening credits are superimposed. This scene dissolves into the second shot: more credits, but this time the tree is on the left and the remainder of the frame is filled with another network of branches. Credits continue as the shot dissolves into a scene of tangled branches emanating from somewhere outside the frame but coming from the left and the right. The final credits are superimposed over the first shot and dissolve into a slowly spinning shot of trees and branches as the narrator begins. This shot, in turn, dissolves into a close-up of a spinning globe in Paul's classroom, and the action of the film begins.

In the first six shots of the film, we are presented with the initial appearance of two important image patterns that express the meaning of Paul's world: trees and balance. Trees, particularly branches of trees, are used to visually express Paul's confusions, the complexity of his thoughts as he tries to understand the meaning of the world around him as well as the strange force that seems to be slowly cutting him off from the world. Trees and branches constantly cut off Paul's vision of the real world, and intrude upon our vision as well, through three-quarters of the film. The last shot of trees (168), an intercut of snow-covered fields and woods, occurs during the inquisition scene. By that time, the voice of the snow has taken possession of Paul, and he resolves his confusions by running away from the adults into his snow-filled room. Once he actively cuts himself off from the complexity of the real world, the visual images of the trees which are used to suggest this complexity are no longer needed.

Up to that point, however, trees and branches actually restrict our vision in many of the shots. For example, while Paul is in the classroom, he thinks of the first morning he failed to hear the postman's steps. When we see the postman for the first time (15), he is seen from Paul's vantage point, a high-angle long shot from his room, and the postman moves up the street toward the boy's house. However, our vision of the postman is restricted because we see him through the interlaced branches of trees that line the street. Even when Paul imagines the postman walking up the street in the snow (35), the next shot, which begins a sequence of snow-covered fields and trees, starts with a high-angle close-up of footprints in snow and continues with a tilt upward, emphasizing the trunks of the trees. The anonymous footprints could be interpreted as the postman's footprints as he leads Paul deeper into the world of branching confusions and mystery. The first exterior shot of Paul looking out of his window (43) includes reflections of branches on the window and the branches seem to surround his head.

On occasion, there are scenes that are not presented from Paul's point of view, but the ubiquitous trees continue to limit our view; thus, we experience the world in much the same way that Paul does, but not through his eyes. Such shots serve to give us a feeling of Paul's world without allowing us to objectify these experiences by thinking that we are seeing the world through his eyes. For example, shot 63 is a ground-level long-shot of the postman walking past the camera. He is partly obscured by an out-of-focus tree in the foreground. But the most telling shot of this kind occurs later, when we watch Paul leave the school on his homeward walk. The sequence begins with a ground-level long-shot of the schoolyard prior to Paul's departure from the building. A group of children is playing kickball; but, again, our vision of the action is obscured by the trunk of a large tree. The trunk of the tree is in the very center of the frame and partially limits our view of the activity. The effect of the shot is somewhat the same as the shot in Antonioni's *L'Eclisse* (1962), when Vittoria and Piero stand on either side of a large stone column that dominates over one-half of the frame. Antonioni holds his shot longer than Kearney does, and Antonioni's shot is more obviously symbolic, but Kearney develops his meaning through an accretion process and his intent is not nearly as obvious. Kearney's shot continues with a slow pan so that we can view more of the action, but the sense of the tree trunk dominates our response.

The next shot has Paul walking out of the building, but it is similiar to the earlier shots of Paul's street in that it is taken from a high angle and the boy is seen through tree branches. As he walks home, one of the shots (106) duplicates the sense of disorientation experienced at the beginning of the film (5) with a low-angle tracking shot of tree trunks and branches that gradually tilts upward 90 degrees. When Paul arrives at the foot of his street, his real world and his fantasy world coalesce: in one shot (113) the street is bare; in the next, it is covered with snow. For the time being, Paul has been captured by his fantasy world, and

Kearney suggests this through a close-up of Paul with a large branch directly overhead (116).

Balance, the other important image pattern initiated in the opening shots, is not visually alluded to as often as trees are, but it is most important to the meaning of the film. Paul retreats into his fantasy world at the end of the film because he is unable to cope with the pressures of living in the real world. We all tend to fantasize to some extent, but most of us are able to maintain a relatively stable personality because we understand the dangers of a fantasy existence. Children, in particular, are tempted to live dream lives because they are constantly frustrated in their attempts to order the chaos of existence in meaningful ways. Fantasy offers a simplistic way of balancing or ordering the chaotic material world. Kearney uses images of balance throughout the film in much the same way he uses branches. At times we experience the branch-like complexity and confusions of the world through a subjective camera that represents Paul's eyes or his mind; at other times we perceive the branches directly. Similarly, some images of balance are subjective and some are objective, but both points of view present images of balanced objects, trees in particular, that suggest Paul's perceptions and his inner state. Whether subjectively or objectively rendered, the images of balance are pleasing to us because we respond to a sense of order. In this way, Kearney allows us to visually experience the same satisfaction that Paul apparently feels in his ordered fantasy world.

As previously noted the images of trees under the opening credits are balanced: 1, tree right; 2, tree left; 3, interlaced branches from left and right; 4, tree right again. Later, this sense of balance is incorporated with the snow-covered trees that suggest his lapse into fantasy. In shots 36–40 Paul imaginatively follows the footsteps of the postman heard outside his bedroom into his own snow-covered world. The camera begins with a close-up of footprints in the snow and tilts up the trunks of trees. We then have shots of a bush in the right foreground, a tilt up to interlaced branches, and a tilt down to the ground. Finally, the next shot is of a snow-covered urn that gradually fills the left of the frame as the camera pans right. Balance is achieved in much the same way later in the film as Paul is again drawn into his fantasy world, symbolized by scenes of snow-covered trees and shrubs. Shot 85 contains a grouping already in balance, possibly suggesting that the pull of the boy's fantasy world is growing stronger. Regardless, the next shot is a view of snow-covered trees at the left of the frame; the following shot a view of other trees at the right of the frame.

The strangest image of balance in the film is found during the sequence of Paul's homeward walk. He walks past a series of steps descending into a field; there are bases on either side of the top of the steps. There is a half of a metal form on each base, some kind of a dragon-like monster, perhaps a griffin. The forms are curiously out of touch with the mundane objects of Paul's world, and they could be understood as another example of the boy's sense of balance to be found in the mysterious forces that are slowly taking over his life.

Apart from the image patterns of trees and balance initiated in the opening shots of the film, the dissolve between shots 5 and 6 serves as a visual metaphor used to represent Paul's state. The spinning trees dissolve into a spinning globe, suggesting that the visual confusion in the trees is like the intellectual confusion that results when one attempts to understand the symbolic geography of the material world. The connection between the trees and the globe is reinforced in shot 13 when the camera zooms in to the polar regions on the map at the front of the classroom. The lines of the rivers and seas remind us of a similar network of lines in the branches of the trees. Snow, of course, is the central symbol in the film, for it represents the fantasy force that is pulling Paul from the material world. His interest in the polar regions is understandable. As the snow falls in his imagination and covers up the external world, it covers up his confusions, the trees, as well. Thus, in shot 40 fir branches are half-buried in snow. Paul gets out of bed in the next shot, but the camera remains focused on his white pillow long enough for us to see the network of the impression made by his head. By the end of the film, snow covers the trees, the pillow, and Paul.

The snow also covers two objects in the boy's room, a small globe and the model of a sailing ship (214, 212). As he tells his parents, "It would be fun to be an explorer, like Peary or Scott, or

Byrd" (80). Paul wants to discover a new world, a world unlike the one he is living in, and he gets glimpses of it throughout the film. It is, as the narrator says, "... irresistible ... miraculous" (82). Ironically, the implication is that at the end of the film Paul is, like Henry Hudson, "... disappointed" (100).

Paul's failure is implied through the white and black imagery in the film. When white and black are used as visual images, white suggests Paul's imaginary world while black represents the world he is trying to escape. Aside from the whiteness of snow in this context, other images are used to suggest the boy's fantasy world. One interesting example has been previously noted, Paul's white pillow with the branch-like impression from his head. The most powerful image of whiteness, aside from the snow itself, is the cut-glass chandelier, probably hanging in one of the downstairs rooms. The chandelier, always lighted, always stark white, is made to stand for the fact that the snow is imaginary and that it is within Paul. As with the amount of snow on the trees, we can chart the strength of his fantasy by noting the sharpness of the shots of the chandelier. The narrator tells us that outside,

> 69 ECU of Paul's eyes. Music
> Narrator: were the bare streets and here

> 70 LS from low angle of lighted cut-glass chandelier ...
> Narrator: inside was the snow

> 71 CU of ... chandelier. Zoom in. Image gradually goes out of focus until ... a blur of light.

The image of the chandelier is intercut at crucial times throughout the rest of the film to remind us that Paul's white world is within himself. The last shot of the chandelier takes place during the "inquisition" scene immediately before the last shot of snow-covered trees, and by that time we only see the bottom half, which is out of focus.

Another image of whiteness is somewhat less powerful but holds interesting dramatic values: Paul's glass of milk. In *Suspicion* (1941), Hitchcock lighted a glass of milk by placing a light bulb inside the glass, and somewhat the same sense of luminousness and import is gained during Paul's scene with his parents at breakfast. When Paul comes to the table he finds the milk waiting for

him. He reaches for it, holds it, stares at it, but does not drink
(48). He slides it across the table towards himself, puts his other
hand around it, holds it, gazes at it, and finally drinks (49–52).
Nearly half a minute of film goes by from the moment he touches
the glass to the time he drinks. During that time his gaze moves
from the mother to the father to the milk. It is a large glass of
milk; Paul seems to wonder if he should drink the white; he seems
uncertain.

Images of blackness or darkness are sometimes used in the film
to suggest Paul's concept of the limitations of the adult world. The
adults, particularly the parents, lack Paul's insights, which are suggested by whiteness; thus, their lives are spent in dark shadows.
The mother is strikingly dressed in black (68) and in the "inquisition" scene in particular the father is seen in shadows with pitch
blackness behind him. Further, the only fade-out within the film
takes place in Paul's bedroom (93). He is considering telling someone about his experiences, but his mother warns him that he will
have to see a doctor if his behavior continues. When she reaches
over him and turns out the light, producing the fade-out, we are
visually told that the adult world of darkness will continue to
prevent Paul from explaining himself. However, the "inquisition"
scene is the most obvious instance of the use of blackness and
darkness to suggest the limitations of the adult world. The scene
is played in a darkened room with very theatrical expressionistic
lighting (138). The acting by the adult players seems poor, but
one could say that the "fake" lighting and the "fake" acting go
hand-in-hand. Since Kearney carefully worked out the visual patterns in the film, one is inclined to give him the benefit of the
doubt here. The scene could be viewed as Paul's subjective interpretation of the adult world. He is interested in discovering what,
in his mind, is a new world; the adults are getting in his way; he
is unable to sympathize with their desire to help him. Hence, they
appear phony to him. As actors, they appear that way to us, but
there are other instances in the film in which Kearney attempts to
have us identify with Paul through a subjective camera.

Black is also used as an ironic image throughout the film. While
the individual trees or spaced groups of trees are generally well
lighted, darkened clusters of trees are often seen, suggesting that

Paul's ultimate understanding will not be whiteness, but blackness (e.g., 103, 168). Given the chandelier shot in which the camera zooms in to an out-of-focus, screen-filling whiteness, one would expect the film to end in the same way, suggesting that Paul had moved into the world of ultimate whiteness. Instead, in the last shot of the film the camera zooms in to an extreme close-up of Paul's face, blurred and out of focus. But the film does not end with a white screen: a dark shadow gradually moves across the screen and the film ends in blackness. Paul did not escape the blackness of the adult world in death or in permanent schizophrenia. Like Henry Hudson, he was disappointed.

But, finally, what were Paul's reasons for his willed decline into a fantasy world? Perhaps Kearney is primarily interested in presenting the viewer with the experience of watching and sympathizing with a youth whose touch with the material world grows progressively weaker until he lapses into death or schizophrenia. On the other hand, there are some puzzling visual images that may suggest causes. To begin with, what is the meaning of Deirdre vigorously scratching the back of her neck? The image occurs first immediately after the postman's knock on the door of Paul's house (24). It occurs the second time in a visual transition from the breakfast table to the classroom. However, most curiously, the dialogue at the breakfast table overlaps the visual cut:

> 56 MCU of Paul, who holds the glass of milk . . .
> Mother (off camera): don't seem to be listening.
> Father (off camera): What
>
> 57 (=26) MCU. Deirdre scratches the back of her neck.
> Father (off camera) in exasperated tones: the devil is it, Paul?

The suggestion here is that Deirdre seems to be bothering Paul, but why Deirdre?

The narrator tells us what we should know about the causes of Paul's condition:

> . . . snow growing heavier each day, muffling the world, hiding the ugly, and deadening increasingly, above all, the steps of the postman. (71)

Deirdre does not represent the world; she is not ugly; obviously she is not the postman. Why Deirdre? It is not Deirdre herself, but Deirdre scratching her neck that is ugly; and this image is joined to the father's question, "What the devil is it, Paul?" Deirdre's very human act serves as a visual example of man's mutability, the gross materiality of the flesh. Paul is reminded that he, too, is human and subject to decay and death, and he wants to escape from that fact by covering himself in a blanket of imaginary whiteness. The coldness of the snow will freeze his living body. Also, Deirdre is not an isolated image of Paul's condition; the urn (39) and the dead mouse (109) suggest the same idea. However, we must not forget that, above all, Paul wants the snow to deaden the steps of the postman. Perhaps the postman is a personification of death. His steps lead into the woods (36), and he leaves dead weeds in his wake (35). Ironically, as in the Preface to John O'Hara's *Appointment in Samarra*, death cannot be avoided by running away. This theme is the very core of the film's pathos.

Visually, the film captures the spirit of a succinct and suggestive short story; the images are selective, often suggestive, and in keeping with the kinds of experiences that shape Paul. However, the spoken narration is not as selective nor as compressed. At times it is richer than the visuals (e.g., 168); on other occasions it is downright misleading (e.g., 104); other times, it is simply redundant (e.g., 184). As in Breer's film, too much is happening on too many levels, and the result tends to be a bit confusing. Some viewers will concentrate on the images and find it impossible to fully understand the subtleties of the language. Many will pay more attention to the language and miss some of the interesting things Kearney is doing with the images. Others may enjoy the film as an impressionistic blur. Further, the complexity of the chronology adds to the problem. As in Resnais' *Hiroshima, Mon Amour* (1959), experience and memory intermingle in the present of the film.

Although Kearney is not nearly as successful, his visual imagery and his narrative chronology are in keeping with the cinematic modernity found in such works as Bunuel's *Belle de Jour* (1967) and Fellini's *Fellini-Satyricon* (1969). While the images and the chronology are needed in the film to suggest the nature of Paul's experience, the spoken narration is too dense. One cannot hope to present a full visual experience and a full verbal experience simultaneously without the risk of muddling both. There are no specific rules for dealing with the relationship between the visual and the verbal in film; the balance between the two forms of communication must be decided upon by the director based on the aesthetic needs of the particular film he is making. However, some directors are more verbally oriented than others, and the verbally oriented directors are always in danger of using language to explain a relationship or an emotion that, given the nature of film, would be more effectively conveyed by the visuals. Kearney would have created a greater sense of succinctness and clarity, and thus would have reflected the formal qualities of a good short story in his film, through a greater compression of the language. While a film should be a marriage of the visual image and the spoken word, the domination of the word over the image seldom works. In "Silent Snow, Secret Snow," Gene Kearney's visuals were seduced by his language.

SUGGESTIONS
FOR PAPERS

Suggestions
for Papers

1. Analyze the "authority figures" (Miss Buell, the doctor, Paul's parents) in Aiken's story and in Kearney's film. Does Kearney make them appear to be more or less complex? Does Kearney or Aiken do more editorializing about the characters?

2. The interpretations of the postman vary from critic to critic. How does Kearney interpret the postman? Which critics share his view?

3. Discuss Paul's homeward walk in both the short story and the film. Do Aiken and Kearney make the same point about the walk? How do they make their points?

4. Identify the major image patterns in Aiken's story. Which ones does Kearney adopt, expand, or delete? Why?

5. What parallels do you find between the schoolroom scene and the inquisition? Are the parallels more numerous in the short story or the film? What is the significance of the parallels?

6. Many critics have read Aiken's short story as a description of an Oedipal complex. Review the essays written by the Freudians and then examine the film. How many of the "Freudian" elements has Kearney included? Has he changed or added any? Does the film reflect a Freudian interpretation?

7. Alienation and the lack of communication between generations are two popular themes in contemporary literature. Discuss these themes in both the short story and the film (you may wish to consider the "two different worlds" motif). Which medium places more emphasis on alienation and lack of communication? How do film and fiction convey these themes?

8. Select a fictional element (character, point-of-view, imagery, etc.) in Aiken's story and suggest how Kearney adapts this element in the film. How would you describe the nature of the adaptation? How would you evaluate it?

9. Three out of the four essays on the film suggest that Kearney was unable or unwilling to deal with the language of the story in cinematic terms. Do you find this to be the case? If so, how successful is the film? If not, how do you account for the essayists' views?

10. Kearney has chosen to eliminate certain passages and ideas that are in the story, while he adds some material of his own to the film. Account for these decisions.

11. Describe Kearney's interpretation of the short story. Which of the story's critics share his view?

12. Describe, as clearly as possible, how Kearney transforms the literary strengths of the story into cinematic strengths.

13. Making use of the materials in this book and your viewing of the film, construct Kearney's theory of film adaptation.

14. Is the film a successful adaptation of the story?